C000022053

OLD WORDS
NEW LIFE

OLD WORDS
NEW LIFE

REFLECTIONS ON 40 KEY OLD TESTAMENT WORDS

DAVID WINTER

Text copyright © David Winter 2005
The author asserts the moral right
to be identified as the author of this work

Published by
The Bible Reading Fellowship
First Floor, Elsfield Hall
15–17 Elsfield Way, Oxford OX2 8FG
Website: www.brf.org.uk

ISBN 1 84101 391 9
First published 2005
10 9 8 7 6 5 4 3 2 1 0
All rights reserved

Acknowledgments
Unless otherwise stated, scripture quotations are taken from The New
Revised Standard Version of the Bible, Anglicized Edition, copyright ©
1989, 1995 by the Division of Christian Education of the National
Council of the Churches of Christ in the USA, and are used by
permission. All rights reserved.

Scripture quotations taken from the *Holy Bible, New International
Version*, copyright © 1973, 1978, 1984 by International Bible Society.
Used by permission of Hodder & Stoughton Limited. All rights
reserved. 'NIV' is a registered trademark of International Bible Society.
UK trademark number 1448790.

Extracts from the Authorized Version of the Bible (The King James
Bible), the rights in which are vested in the Crown, are reproduced by
permission of the Crown's patentee, Cambridge University Press.

A catalogue record for this book is available from the British Library

Printed and bound in Great Britain by
Bookmarque, Croydon

Contents

INTRODUCTION

I wonder how you think of the Old Testament? Blood and thunder, disgusting violence (sometimes not only condoned but apparently ordered by God), highly improbable stories, some extremely unpleasant characters—in fact, a bit of a turn-off? Or, if you are rather more devout, the poetry of the Psalms, the wisdom of Proverbs, the grandeur of the prophecies of Isaiah, and the constant promise of an eventual day of justice and peace, when the lion will lie down with the lamb? All are true; all are elements of this amazing collection of books, written and compiled over a period of almost a thousand years. Above and beyond that, here is a vision of God and a record of the way one tribe and people came to experience him in a unique way through the long story of the birth of a nation.

The title 'Old Testament' rather hides that important truth, as though this is the obsolete version, how things used to be, now superseded by the spanking new modern version, the 'New Testament'. Sometimes it helps if we call this collection of books 'the Hebrew scriptures', because that helps to emphasize exactly what they were and are. These were the scriptures of Jesus, of the apostles, of the early Church. That's why, as the 'New' Testament began to be written, it is so obviously a sequel rather than a replacement. To read the New Testament without any knowledge of the Old Testament would be like starting a novel in the middle and expecting to understand it properly. Christians ignore the Hebrew scriptures at their peril—the very serious peril of frequently getting the wrong end of the stick. How, for instance, could anyone hope to understand the epistle to the Hebrews who had not read Leviticus? It simply wouldn't make sense.

I'm not so deluded as to imagine that one short book can provide its readers with all the keys to the various compartments of the Old Testament. What I hope it will do is whet some appetites, and also make it just a little easier to see the Hebrew scriptures as they are. By concentrating on the meaning of 40 key words, rather than long passages, I want to help the person who turns to this amazing anthology of stories, poems and ideas with linguistic 'tools', as it were, to get into its special way of thinking. Just because a word appears in the Gospels, say, (which were written in Greek) and also in Deuteronomy (which was written in Hebrew) doesn't mean that it is saying the same thing. For example, there is no Hebrew word that means precisely what the New Testament means by 'faith', and there is no New Testament word that precisely conveys what the lovely Hebrew word *hesed* means—the word which the King James Version beautifully translated 'loving-kindness'.

This book can be used in two ways. You can, if you wish, read it straight through, perhaps a day at a time, reflecting on each word and absorbing its distinctive meaning for the writers and readers of the Hebrew scriptures. Or, just as validly, you can put it on the shelf beside your copy of the Bible, and when you are reading a passage from the Old Testament refer to it to see if there is a section on a particular word that occurs there. To make that easier, the 40 words are set out in alphabetical order. There is, of course, a 'third way' of using it, if you are a preacher or leader of a Bible study group. I hope that there is material here that will help when you are preparing a talk or sermon, or trying to grapple with a particularly elusive Old Testament concept.

There is one other suggestion as to how this book can be used. Some readers might find it helpful to read the very last chapter, on 'Yahweh', before they read the rest. At least that will help to explain the presence in the text of a name which is unfamiliar, as yet, to many readers of the Bible, but occurs more frequently in the scriptures than any other proper noun.

Whichever way you choose to use it, my hope is that the book will provide something of a stimulus to the reading of the Hebrew Bible, the Bible of Jesus—the book from which he quoted while hanging on the cross—and the scriptures which the apostle Paul called 'inspired by God' (2 Timothy 3:16). It may indeed be 'old', but, like many old things, it is infinitely valuable.

The Hebrew scriptures

Although the order of the books is different, the Hebrew scriptures are virtually identical to what Christians call the 'Old Testament'. They had developed into their current form by the second century BC, and are divided into three sections—the law, the prophets and the writings. The oldest section, the law (or the 'Pentateuch'), was complete in its present form and accepted as having divine authority rather earlier, by the time of Ezra and Nehemiah (fifth century BC). Because of the way the books are divided, there are only 36 books in the Hebrew scriptures, compared to the 39 in the Christian Old Testament, even though the material is identical. The prophets are placed in the Hebrew canon after Kings (which is one, not two books) and before Psalms and the other wisdom books. Chronicles (again one book, not two) is, rather strangely, the last book of the Hebrew scriptures.

The books of the Hebrew scriptures are as follows:

- The law (the Pentateuch)
  - Genesis
  - Exodus
  - Leviticus
  - Numbers
  - Deuteronomy

- The prophets
  - Isaiah
  - Jeremiah
  - Ezekiel
  - Hosea
  - Joel
  - Amos
  - Obadiah
  - Jonah
  - Micah

- Nahum
- Habakkuk
- Zephaniah
- Haggai
- Zechariah
- Malachi

• The writings (historical)
  - Joshua
  - Judges
  - Samuel
  - Kings

• The writings (wisdom)
  - Psalms
  - Proverbs
  - Job
  - Song of Solomon
  - Ruth
  - Lamentations
  - Ecclesiastes

(The following historical books are placed after the wisdom writings)
  - Esther
  - Daniel
  - Ezra
  - Nehemiah
  - Chronicles

If you are interested in exploring the separate books of the Old Testament further, look out for *The People's Bible Commentary*, published by BRF. The series is almost complete, and offers a daily readings approach that brings together both personal devotion and reflective study. Ask your local Christian bookshop for details, or look at BRF's website: www.brf.org.uk.

I

ATONEMENT

For on this day atonement shall be made for you, to cleanse you; from all your sins you shall be clean before the Lord. It is a sabbath of complete rest to you, and you shall deny yourselves; it is a statute for ever. The priest who is anointed and consecrated as priest in his father's place shall make atonement, wearing the linen vestments, the holy vestments. He shall make atonement for the sanctuary, and he shall make atonement for the tent of meeting and for the altar, and he shall make atonement for the priests and for all the people of the assembly. This shall be an everlasting statute for you, to make atonement for the people of Israel once in the year for all their sins.

LEVITICUS 16:30–34a

After a particularly inept month or two of mail deliveries, with postal strikes, go-slows, bad weather and a certain degree of incompetence all round, the chief executive of the Royal Mail wrote to his customers. It was an apologetic, almost grovelling letter, admitting many faults and failures. They couldn't, he explained, offer individual compensation, but as a gesture (a sign of true repentance?) they would be donating one million pounds to the British Olympic Fund. He didn't use the word, of course, but what he was doing—in theological language—was trying to atone for their sin by making a sacrifice.

That offers one picture of atonement. In truth, the postal failures, while irritating and irksome, hardly constituted mortal sin, nor did they (outside the ranks of the Royal Mail employees) destroy valuable and valued relationships. And the donation to the Olympic Fund, while probably welcome in its coffers, was hardly a 'sacrifice', being funded, presumably, by the profits the Royal Mail had made from its customers. Still, the principle was there. There had been fault. One party was guilty, the other innocent. Atonement had been made.

And that is the principle of atonement. Sin matters. Forgiveness doesn't come on the cheap. There is a price to pay for it. The paying of that price is the evidence of guilt acknowledged and therefore the key to forgiveness. The sinner has 'atoned'—paid the price.

This principle can be seen all through the social and moral commandments set out in what is called the Mosaic law (the law given through Moses). In some cases—injury to a pregnant woman, for instance, or to a neighbour's ox—atonement is made by a financial penalty. In other cases, the sacrifice of an animal is required in order to achieve atonement. This atonement, the law makes clear, is two-fold: between the offender and the person wronged, and between the offender and God.

It is a commonplace of human experience that lies, dishonesty, unfaithfulness, cruelty and selfishness can and do destroy valued and valuable relationships. However much love there is on one side, actions of this kind, what the Bible calls 'sin', can create an unbridgeable gap between two people.

What is true of human experience, in the relationship of one person to another, is also true in the relationship between God and people. Sin can destroy the relationship between a God of love and holiness and his less than loving and holy creatures. This is not due to a failure of God's love, but because what is utterly holy cannot be united with what is evil.

However, God has never been prepared simply to leave it at that—indeed, if he had, he would have committed himself to a lonely eternity in an empty heaven! From the earliest times, the Hebrew scriptures speak of this principle of 'atonement', the means by which a reconciliation can be effected. This traditionally involved sacrifices of animals: sheep, goats, bulls. In offering a sacrifice, the one who was seeking reconciliation was paying a price (though the modern reader may feel that the animal paid the greater one!). That price was more than a million pounds to the Olympic Fund. It was blood, and the great altar in the temple must have been blood-soaked every day, as thousands of such sacrifices were made.

The passage above is part of the description in Leviticus of the Day of Atonement (*Yom Kippur*), still today a solemn occasion in the Jewish calendar, though, in the absence of a temple, no longer marked by animal sacrifice. Now, it is the day in the year when Jews remember, confess and repent of their sins, individual and collective, and seek God's mercy. In Leviticus, however, it involved a dramatic and visually compelling ritual, conducted by the high priest for that year. On the Day of Atonement, and only then, he would enter the Most Holy Place, the very heart of the temple and the place of the symbolic 'presence of the Lord'. Before entering, he would have gone through various rites of purification, donned the sacred vestments and offered sacrifice for his own sins. He also took two goats. One was sacrificed to cleanse the holy place and the tent of meeting (the tabernacle) from 'the sins of the people'. He laid his hands on the head of the second one and would 'confess over it all the iniquities of the people of Israel, and all their transgressions, all their sins' (Leviticus 16:21). That goat, the so-called 'scapegoat', was then led away to a barren region and 'set free in the wilderness' to 'bear on itself all their iniquities' (v. 22).

On the Day of Atonement, in this solemn and dramatic way, the sins and iniquities of priests and people were cleansed and forgiven through the shedding of blood, and through the transference of guilt to a scapegoat. In this way, their sins were atoned for and their relationship with God restored. However odd, even bizarre, we may find these rites and rituals, at least the people could understand that sin mattered because it damaged their covenant relationship with God, that it required atonement and also that God welcomed back those who confessed and repented their sins. Indeed, so solemn and awesome were these rites, it is hard to believe that at least on that day of the year the priests and people were not united in deep and genuine contrition. It was the blood of a bull and a goat that was sprinkled on the mercy seat, the altar and the tabernacle, but it was the open admission of guilt on the part of the people that made atonement possible. In the manner of a sacrament, the rituals were the outward and visible 'sign'; the inward grace was repentance.

The ritual of the Day of Atonement is considered in detail by the writer of the epistle to the Hebrews in the New Testament. He describes what happened in the temple and the Holy of Holies on that particular day of the year, but concludes, somewhat dismissively, that 'it is impossible for the blood of bulls and goats to take away sins' (10:4). He sees these rites as being concerned simply with the ritual purification of 'the flesh', whereas the sacrifice of Jesus, the 'high priest of the good things that have come' (9:11a), which he compares to them, is able to 'purify our *conscience* from dead works to worship the living God' (9:14b).

Atonement, then, may be an essentially Old Testament concept, yet according to the New Testament writers its true and deepest meaning was only fulfilled in the offering of Jesus, 'whom God put forward as a sacrifice of atonement by his blood, effective through faith' (Romans 3:25a). It may not be a word we use very often, but it conveys a deep and reassuring meaning. That which has been separated can be brought together again—though only at a cost. When we are powerless to atone for our own sins and failures, God pays the cost of our atonement. In the picture-language of Leviticus, the Son of God became both the sacrifice for sins and the scapegoat, bearing them away for ever.

A reflection

'Scapegoats' are a regular if sad element in life—at work, in politics, even in the Church: the innocent person who is meant to carry the blame for the failures of another. How remarkable, then, that the Lamb of God became our scapegoat when, as John the Baptist put it, he took away the sin of the world (John 1:29b).

2

BLESSING

The angel of the Lord called to Abraham a second time from
heaven, and said, 'By myself I have sworn, says the Lord:
Because you have done this, and have not withheld your son,
your only son, I will indeed bless you, and I will make your
offspring as numerous as the stars of heaven and as the sand
that is on the seashore. And your offspring shall possess the
gate of their enemies, and by your offspring shall all the nations
of the earth gain blessing for themselves, because you have
obeyed my voice.'
GENESIS 22:15–18

'Bless' and 'blessing' are common enough words, but it's
remarkably hard, even in English, to pin down their precise
meaning. 'Oh, bless you!' people say, or describe someone as a real
'blessing' to them. The extent to which all this blessing has
anything to do with God, or what the Bible might mean by the
word, will of course vary according to the beliefs of the speaker. Yet
we can at least say that 'blessing' and 'bless' are words of gratitude
and enrichment; we intend the one blessed to be affirmed by it.

In the Hebrew scriptures, the words 'bless' and 'blessing' are
very common, as even a cursory glance at the concordance will
confirm, though they are not always used in the same way. Clearly,
the most important blessing is that given by God. The passage
above, God's great covenant blessing on Abraham and his
descendants, is a good example. God blesses people, as he does
here—not just Abraham's descendants, but all the nations of
the earth, who will gain blessing through them—but he also
blesses animals (Genesis 1:22), land (Deuteronomy 26:15), houses

(Proverbs 3:33), crops (Deuteronomy 7:13), bread and water (Exodus 23:25), work (Deuteronomy 28:8) and the sabbath (Genesis 2:3).

But people also bless. A familiar example is Isaac's blessing of Jacob (Genesis 27:27)—a blessing which was irrevocable, even though obtained by deceit. Sometimes such blessings, as in this case, were solemn and binding, virtually the equivalent of an oath in a court of law. Sometimes they were part of a religious rite, as when the priests blessed the people (1 Samuel 2:20). In other cases, they simply expressed one human being's desire to invoke divine favour on someone else (Genesis 47:7)—probably the equivalent of the modern 'Bless you!'

People don't only bless other people; they sometimes bless things, especially articles of religious or sacrificial significance (1 Samuel 9:13). Christians will remember that Jesus blessed the bread and fish at the feeding of the five thousand and the bread and wine at the last supper.

All of these examples show how varied is the usage of the verb to 'bless' and the abstract noun 'blessing'. Yet there is a common thread in the biblical use of the word. In virtually every case, it implies the invoking of God's favour and the hope that such invocation will change the situation, the person or even the thing for the better. Indeed, if we remove that element of divine involvement, it's hard to see what point there is in blessing anybody or anything.

There are two further uses of the word in the Old Testament, neither of which contradicts what we have already considered, but which extend the word's meaning or apply it in a different way. One—very common in the Psalms, for instance—is the idea of human beings blessing God. 'Bless the Lord, O my soul, and all that is within me, bless his holy name' (Psalm 103:1). In Christian liturgy, we often say: 'Blessed be God for ever'. Clearly human beings cannot bestow favour or goodness on God, who is himself the source of favour and goodness, so what can we mean when we speak of blessing the Lord? The general view of the experts is that these blessings of God are expressions of praise, worship or thanksgiving, rather than invocations of favour or goodness.

That brings us to the second example of an extension of the fundamental idea of blessing: those whom the Lord blesses are truly happy. In the Old Testament, a different Hebrew word (*asre*) is sometimes translated 'blessed', but in this case its true meaning is 'happy' or 'content'. In the same way, the Greek word *makarios* in the New Testament is often translated 'blessed', though its literal meaning is 'happy' (the most familiar example is in the Beatitudes: Matthew 5:3–11). In fact, happiness or contentment are the natural consequence of God's blessing, just as neglect or rejection of his blessing lead to misery and discontent.

As we read the Hebrew scriptures today, the overwhelming impression is of a people who sought (even if they too often failed) to live their lives under the covenant blessing of God. They knew that there was nothing good that didn't ultimately come from him, and that the safest, happiest and most secure place to be was within his blessing. 'The Lord has been mindful of us; he will bless us... May you be blessed by the Lord, who made heaven and earth' (Psalm 115:12, 15).

To be blessed by God is the greatest privilege available to human beings, because his blessing conveys all that he is: wisdom, holiness, justice, mercy and, perhaps above all, love. To seek his blessing, therefore, is simply the highest calling for humankind.

A reflection

The Lord bless you and keep you;
the Lord make his face to shine upon you,
and be gracious to you;
the Lord lift up his countenance upon you,
and give you peace.

NUMBERS 6:24–26

3

CHOOSE

I call heaven and earth to witness against you today that I have set before you life and death, blessings and curses. Choose life so that you and your descendants may live, loving the Lord your God, obeying him, and holding fast to him; for that means life to you and length of days, so that you may live in the land that the Lord swore to give to your ancestors, to Abraham, to Isaac, and to Jacob.

DEUTERONOMY 30:19–20

The whole story of the Bible is full of choices: human ones, and God's ones. The need to 'choose' is implicit in humanity. People are God's creatures but, by his design, creatures with the right and privilege of choice. Back in the Garden of Eden, in that strange story which sets the scene for the whole of the scriptures, Adam and Eve had a choice to make: to obey God's apparently arbitrary command not to eat the fruit of a certain tree, or to exercise their 'right' of choice and eat it. There is something touchingly human about their decision to ignore the rule and try the fruit. However much we may deplore it, we know that like them we too would have found it almost irresistible. Human beings have been doing it ever since— not literally eating forbidden fruit, but deciding that we know better than our creator and following our own inclinations. And thereby hangs the whole sorry tale...

Life is made up of decisions: trivial ones, and life-changing ones. We choose what clothes to wear in the morning, what to eat for lunch, which film to see or book to borrow from the library. But we also choose a career, or to marry, or to emigrate—huge choices that affect everything else for the rest of our lives. We also choose what set of beliefs or principles to live by, what to make our priorities and goals, whether we believe in God or not. If life is made up of choices, then it's as well to realize how vitally important some of them are.

Sometimes we feel overwhelmed by choice. I must admit that I find a long menu in a restaurant very daunting. On the whole I prefer à la carte. Again, it's true of important things—which of hundreds of courses to choose at college, which of hundreds of jobs to apply for. It can be equally difficult, however, when there are only two choices, as anyone who has been on a jury can testify: guilty, or not guilty, with all that your decision will mean to the life of the accused.

Yet, difficult as decisions can be, we would not wish to be deprived of the right to choose. God has made us morally auto-nomous, which is a complicated way of saying that he doesn't force or compel us into good behaviour, but leaves us free to choose. It is part of the dignity of humanity, a faint reflection of his own right to choose in matters relating to his creation. We are not angels, nor are we robots programmed to do his will. He made us to love and obey him freely, without compulsion.

Of course, that is a huge responsibility for his human creatures to bear, and time and again in the long story of the human quest for God people have made wrong choices, like that couple in the Garden of Eden. Each of us could speak of times when we are aware that we have acted against God's will—made the 'wrong choice', as it were.

The passage above is from the final discourse of Moses to the people he had led to the borders of the Promised Land. In categorical terms, he set before them the choice: life or death; blessing or curse. To hold fast to their God and to obey him would bring life and blessing; to stray from him and ignore or break his laws would bring death and a curse. He wanted them to know what was at stake, and his plea is eloquent and stark: choose life!

Choosing between good and evil is a fundamental human responsibility. Of course, many factors, some outside our control, may influence our choice: upbringing, nurture, rejection, abuse. Yet the Old Testament asserts over and over again that each person is responsible for his or her own actions, and that that responsibility is God-given. There comes a point in a child's development when, as Isaiah puts it, 'he knows how to refuse the evil and choose the good' (7:15b). In the end, it is demeaning to excuse our behaviour on the grounds of circumstance or upbringing. God 'the Judge of all the earth' (Genesis 18:25) knows all about them, and will make due allowance. To take away the dignity of choice from a person, however, would be to make them less than human, less than what the creator intended them to be.

It is a challenging call, echoing throughout the scriptures. 'Choose life!'

A reflection

How can we know how to 'refuse the evil and choose the good' in our daily lives, in decisions great and small? The classic answers still hold true, surely: conscience, prayer, Bible, honest and careful reflection. Wonderfully, when we make a wrong choice and face the consequences, there is also the grace of forgiveness and God's help to make a fresh start.

4

CHOSEN

For you are a people holy to the Lord your God; the Lord your God has chosen you out of all the peoples on earth to be his people, his treasured possession. It was not because you were more numerous than any other people that the Lord set his heart on you and chose you—for you were the fewest of all peoples. It was because the Lord loved you and kept the oath that he swore to your ancestors, that the Lord has brought you out with a mighty hand, and redeemed you from the house of slavery, from the hand of Pharaoh king of Egypt.

DEUTERONOMY 7:6–8

In the last chapter, we looked at the verb 'to choose', and considered the privilege and responsibility of human choice. Now we turn to another part of the same verb, 'chosen'. This occurs equally frequently in the Hebrew scriptures, and considers the question of choice from the reverse side, as it were.

When Moses confronted Pharaoh and demanded that he let God's people, then slaves in Egypt, go free, a fascinating battle of wills ensued. The king had no desire to let these useful tools of his kingdom go off, and made that clear, but doing so put him on a collision course not just with Moses—who was he, after all?—but with the God of Abraham, Isaac and Jacob.

As the struggle develops, we find Pharaoh's reaction described in three different and yet connected phrases. Sometimes the chronicler of Exodus says that 'The Lord hardened Pharaoh's heart', sometimes that 'Pharaoh's heart was hardened' and sometimes that 'Pharaoh hardened his heart' (see, for example, Exodus 7:13; 8:15; 8:19; 14:8). In other words, God chose to harden Pharaoh's heart, or Pharaoh's heart was hardened by circumstances and events, or Pharaoh chose himself to harden his heart. All three describe the same result, of course, but they look at it from different angles.

For the biblical writers—all of them—nothing happens in the world without God's involvement. He is its creator, and he is in ultimate charge of events in it. For them, to think otherwise would be to turn God into a powerless deity, for all the world like the gods of the heathen. However, they also recognize what we were looking at in the last chapter, the human responsibility before God of choice, and that our choices, added up and put together, also change events. In that sense, we are either co-operators with the divine will or opponents of it, even if only momentarily.

In all of this it is God, not humans, who makes the ultimate choice. That is the crux of the matter for the biblical writers. We don't dictate to God, but either choose to do what he wills or sadly choose to reject it. We make the choice, as we saw in the last chapter, but it is the Lord almighty who sets the consequences of our choice. In the end, God's 'choice' prevails. How could it be otherwise?

This leads to a kind of tension, which Christians have always been aware of in the scriptures. What is the connection, if any, between my choice, which seems so important and final to me, and God's will, which always has the final word? Am I really free to choose at all, or is it only God who has any true choice to make? If it's only God, why does he choose to bless some people and not others—because that is how it seems to be to us. Why, for instance, did God choose the Jews—which implies that everybody else was not chosen?

That question is answered, in God's terms, in the passage above: he chose them not because they were more numerous or powerful than the other nations, but because he loved them and because he kept the promise he had made to Abraham. In other words, he loved them not because they were 'lovable', but because he is love, and because he is a God who by his very nature keeps his promises—is 'faithful', in biblical language.

The same question is answered in another way by saying that God's choices are always good, and their intention is the good of his whole creation. The Israelites were chosen by God, confirmed by the promises he made to Abraham, but the intention was nothing less than blessing for the whole world (Genesis 18:18). In his wisdom, God would bless all the nations through the people he had chosen. That in itself introduces an element of risk into the equation, because this high purpose was entrusted, as it were, to a very fallible bunch of human beings. God chose, and I suppose we could say that he watched over the progress of his choice. His interventions were very occasional, but as the story unfolded they were also crucial in keeping those chosen people to their calling.

The Hebrew scriptures are also full of references to individual people who were 'chosen' by God for a particular purpose, men and women such as Gideon, Moses, Deborah, Samuel and the great king David. What this tells us is that God works out his purposes by many different means and by many unique individuals (some of whom, like Samson, were not outstandingly 'good' people by any standards!). This is not favouritism, like the captain of the team picking his personal friends for the squad, but a way of demonstrating that it is not people's skills, or eloquence, or wisdom that God needs. If he has chosen them, that will be qualification enough. As we have seen, God did not choose the people of Israel because of any gift or quality which they possessed, but because they would fit his purpose. As they were to discover, to be God's 'chosen' is not necessarily a matter to be boasted about. 'You only have I known of all the families of the earth; therefore I will punish you for all your iniquities' (Amos 3:2). Therefore!

Those who are 'chosen' for any task, great or small, will be aware of the weight of responsibility which that places on them. Israel's greatest sin was constantly to forget that. Israel's greatest glory was that in the end their Messiah was to assume the responsibility which they had so heedlessly discarded.

A reflection

'You did not choose me but I chose you', Jesus told his first apostles (John 15:16a). The Gospels tell us that Jesus said 'Follow me' to the men he had chosen as his disciples, but they still had to get up, leave their boats, the tax booth or the harvest field, and respond to his call. The Lord 'chooses'—and then we 'choose' to respond.

5

COMMANDMENT

The law of the Lord is perfect,
reviving the soul;
the decrees of the Lord are sure,
making wise the simple;
the precepts of the Lord are right,
rejoicing the heart;
the commandment of the Lord is clear,
enlightening the eyes.

PSALM 19:7–8

You won't get far in the Hebrew scriptures before encountering the word 'commandment'. In fact, the people of Israel were defined by two things: their covenant relationship with God, and the law of God which they were to observe as their side of the agreement. The law—the commandments, the precepts, the decrees (the synonyms fall over themselves in Hebrew)—is central to the Jewish religion. At first, it may well have been simply the Decalogue, the Ten Commandments given to Moses on Sinai—on 'tablets of stone, written with the finger of God' (Exodus 31:18). The extensions, applications and refinements of those principles were developed into a massive code of moral, ritual and social law, however, covering just about every aspect of life. This body of law can be found in Exodus, Leviticus, Numbers and Deuteronomy, which together with Genesis make up what Jewish people call *torah*, which means law, instruction, teaching. It's interesting that quite a large part of these books consists of narrative rather than legal directives, yet in a way the 'story' is also part of the teaching.

The Ten Commandments are undoubtedly the quintessence of

the whole law, though clearly they are not case or statute law, of the kind that could be enforced in court. How would you ever get a conviction for 'coveting' for instance? (And if you did, who would be left unpunished?) They begin with the covenant relationship which is their very basis: 'I am the Lord your God, who brought you out of the land of Egypt, out of the house of slavery' (Exodus 20:2). All that follows rests on that relationship.

The Ten Commandments set out core principles: the sovereignty of God, the duty of worship, the importance of family and marriage, the place of the sabbath-rest, as well as prohibiting behaviour which is universally condemned, such as murder and theft. The statutes and regulations which feature particularly in Leviticus and Numbers could be seen as elaborations of those principles.

Two things need to be said about God's commandments as they are found in the Old Testament—two things which may serve to correct an impression which readers of the New Testament might erroneously pick up.

The first is that the commandments of God were a gift and blessing to God's people, rather than a burden. They are the 'teaching'. They set out a way of life which would bring to those people fulfilment and happiness. The enormously long Psalm 119 makes the point over and over again. 'Happy are those... who walk in the law of the Lord' (v. 1), 'Happy are those who keep his decrees' (v. 2), 'I treasure your word in my heart' (v. 11), 'I delight in the way of your decrees' (v. 14), 'Open my eyes, so that I may behold wondrous things out of your law' (v. 18), 'Lead me in the path of your commandments, for I delight in it' (v. 35)—and so on and on, right through to verse 174: 'Your law is my delight'. No evidence here of reluctant obedience or miserable submission to a burdensome set of rules. To live in the way of God's command-ments is indeed life and health. That is the central message of the Hebrew scriptures.

The second thing to notice is how firmly the law is set in a relationship. This is not a matter of a remote tyrant, or even a benevolent monarch, imposing his laws on a reluctant people. Israel entered into a unique relationship with *Yahweh*, the Lord God, and within that relationship an essential element was willing obedience to his good and generous law. In other words, all of this took place between those who were in a covenant relationship—a theme we shall look at in the next chapter.

A fair analogy would be marriage, which is also a covenant relationship. Freely and willingly a man and a woman surrender certain individual rights and privileges in the interests of a greater good, their covenant love for each other. To commit adultery, for instance, would be to break the covenant, which is based on a promise of life-long fidelity. This is not enslavement or bondage, because it is freely entered into, but it is utterly and completely binding. There are, as one young man said to me at a wedding interview, absolutely no escape clauses. The commandments of God are like that. They were freely entered into by the people of Israel and in their better moments they enjoyed the blessings and benefits of them. It is a sad commentary on human nature that the history of the nation from Sinai onwards is in fact the history of failure both to keep the commandments of God and to reap their benefits.

There was another bitter, and typically human, consequence of the gift of the law, and it is this which Paul and others in the New Testament—including Jesus himself—were strong to denounce. That is the human tendency to turn a vision into a system. Over the centuries, the Torah was subject to the tireless work of scribes, elaborating and interpreting its every word. This became the system of law which prevailed at the time of Jesus—the work of the scribes and teachers of the law for whom he had so little time. Under their intrusive fingers the teaching which was meant to delight became a tiresome obsession with trivia. Precisely what must one tithe? Should it include such common wayside plants as mint? Why, yes, they said, of course. But while loading minute observance on one side, they also invented (in the manner of lawyers throughout history) any number of escape clauses and subtle ruses for evading the genuine thrust of the teaching.

That—not the 'law of the Lord [which] is perfect' (Psalm 19:7)—

was what Jesus denounced and Paul railed against. Like every other good thing we receive, God's commandments are his gracious gift to his people.

A reflection

It was God's grace that saved Israel, when by his own power he brought them out of slavery. The law was given to be the light for their path through life. It is by grace that Christians hope for salvation, and God's moral laws still stand before us as markers for our journey of faith.

6

COVENANT

You stand assembled today, all of you, before the Lord your God—
the leaders of your tribes, your elders, and your officials, all the
men of Israel, your children, your women, and the aliens who are
in your camp, both those who cut your wood and those who draw
your water—to enter into the covenant of the Lord your God,
sworn by an oath, which the Lord your God is making with you
today; in order that he may establish you today as his people, and
that he may be your God, as he promised you and as he swore to
your ancestors, to Abraham, to Isaac, and to Jacob. I am making
this covenant, sworn by an oath, not only with you who stand here
with us today before the Lord our God, but also with those who
are not here with us today.
DEUTERONOMY 29:10–15

Most people today are at least aware of 'covenants', though seldom
if ever in the terms Moses is proposing here. Our covenants are
either financial (I 'covenant' to pay a charity a certain sum of money,
the Treasury 'covenants' to repay them the tax on it) or matrimonial.
In the marriage service a man and a woman enter into a solemn
covenant of faithful, lifelong love. In both cases promises are made
which are serious, solemn and binding. A covenant, in other words,
is not just a pious hope or a wish, but a strong commitment, in
some cases enforceable by law.

   These words are those of Moses—part of his farewell discourse to
the people of Israel, which makes up virtually the whole of the book
of Deuteronomy. He is at pains to remind them that they are a
covenant people. All that had happened to them since they left
Egypt they owed to the Lord. It was his hand and power that freed

them, his generosity which fed them in the wilderness and gave them victory over the hostile tribes of the region. At Horeb God not only gave them a law, but he engaged them in a solemn and binding covenant. He would be their God. They would be his people. There was, however, one condition to this covenant, unlike the covenant he had made with Abraham, which was unconditional. They were to keep his commandments—they would be for ever the people of the law of the Lord (see, for instance, Jeremiah 31:33).

If we were to compare this covenant with modern parallels, it would fall somewhere between the financial covenant (with conditions and penalties) and the marriage covenant (which is purely a covenant of love). God had made them his people, as we saw earlier, not because they were particularly good or holy, but because of his undeserved favour—what the Bible calls 'grace'. 'Know then, that the Lord your God is not giving you this good land to occupy because of your righteousness; for you are a stubborn people', Moses told them (Deuteronomy 9:6). He made them his because of his love (see Deuteronomy 4:37) and not because of their deservingness.

Yet this stubborn and rebellious people were called to witness to the nations the justice and righteousness of God, by living by the demanding standards of his law. They were to love him before any created thing. They were to honour and reverence his name. They were to observe the sacred sabbath, honour their parents, and live honest, truthful and faithful lives. In this way they would maintain their side of the covenant. For his part, God would be their God— yes, even if they failed, he would remain faithful. 'Because the Lord your God is a merciful God, he will neither abandon you nor destroy you; he will not forget the covenant with your ancestors that he swore to them' (Deuteronomy 4:31).

Such was the covenant with Israel, a rich and generous provision for the people so long as they walked in the way of the Lord's commandments. The later prophets of Israel made it very clear that God was not all that bothered about the ritual and ceremonial commandments, which the people were generally careful to observe, even while playing fast and loose with the moral ones. What he desired was inward obedience, pure hearts, clean hands: 'For I desire steadfast love and not sacrifice, the knowledge of God rather than burnt-offerings' (Hosea 6:6).

The covenant with Israel, Paul tells us, has never been abrogated ('For the gifts and the calling of God are irrevocable': Romans 11:29). What has happened is that a new covenant between God and people has been introduced, what Jesus called 'the new covenant in my blood' (Luke 22:20). This, like the covenant with Israel, is based on a relationship of love and dependence. It is, like the covenant with Abraham, unconditional, entered into on the human side by acceptance of the gracious gift as an act of dependent faith. Unlike the later covenant with Moses, it does not require observance of ritual and ceremonial law, but by the nature of the relationship it creates it is clearly intended to lead its human participants into lives which mirror the goodness, justice and holiness of God.

'Covenant' is a lovely word. It speaks of two parties coming together in agreement, making binding promises with the intention of fulfilling them. When attached to a relationship, it makes it secure and reliable. When the extra ingredient of love is added, we have what must be the perfect covenant—two parties, one will, one heart, one goal.

A reflection

Our God is a God of covenant love, who graciously draws people into this relationship of security, trust and faithfulness. There is no higher calling than to live within that relationship.

7

FAITHFUL

Know therefore that the Lord your God is God, the faithful God who maintains covenant loyalty with those who love him and keep his commandments, to a thousand generations, and who repays in their own person those who reject him. He does not delay but repays in their own person those who reject him. Therefore, observe diligently the commandment—the statutes, and the ordinances—that I am commanding you today. If you heed these ordinances, by diligently observing them, the Lord your God will maintain with you the covenant loyalty that he swore to your ancestors.

DEUTERONOMY 7:9–12

Love the Lord, all you his saints. The Lord preserves the faithful.

PSALM 31:23a

There is no Hebrew word that is exactly equivalent to the Greek word translated as 'faith' in the New Testament. To believe in God or not to believe weren't real options in the ancient world. Everybody believed; the only question was the identity of the God in whom they believed. However, faith, in the sense of personal trust in God, was certainly also present. Clearly, Abraham trusted God, and so did David, Elijah and many, many others.

What is very important in the Hebrew scriptures, however, is the notion of faithfulness. God is faithful. He maintains 'the covenant loyalty he swore to... [their] ancestors' (Deuteronomy 7:12). Just think of all the metaphors: God as rock, as high tower, as the hills around Jerusalem. He is the one who can never be moved, unshakeable in his reliability. Even when his people turn their backs on him he cannot deny his nature; he still remains faithful. In a shifting and changing world, where people constantly betray you and let you down, there is one—and only one—upon whom we can rely, the constant, strong and faithful Lord God.

In a sense, God's faithfulness is always more important than how much faith I have. Even the strongest human faith probably falters at times—look at Elijah on Mount Carmel! The man who had boldly defied the weak king, Ahab, and his evil wife, Jezebel, suddenly crumpled into self-pity. He fled to the wilderness, pleading with God to take away his life, because he was no better than his ancestors. Everything had gone wrong. His whole ministry had been a failure. 'The Israelites have forsaken your covenant, thrown down your altars, and killed your prophets with the sword. I alone am left, and they are seeking my life, to take it away' (1 Kings 19:10).

Human faith can and does falter, but that does not affect God's faithfulness, as Elijah soon discovered. We change; we are subject to moods of despair or exhilaration. God is pictured by the psalmist as sitting in the heavens above all this nonsense, unchanging and unchangeable, the faithful God of his people. The Hebrew word (*aman*) means 'reliable, constant'—qualities we value in our friends or colleagues when we find them. Supremely, they are the qualities God possesses.

That brings us to the other use of faithful, which is found in the second, brief passage of scripture above. 'The Lord preserves the faithful' (Psalm 31:23a). God is faithful, and longs for his people to be, or to become, faithful. This does not mean that he wants them to believe in him more strongly (they already believed, in an intellectual sense), but he wants their devotion to him to be constant and reliable, not a matter of moods or feelings.

The most consistent complaint God had about the people of Israel was their unfaithfulness. Amos, Micah and Hosea make this their constant theme. Hosea, especially, with his harrowing pictures of an unfaithful wife, shows in detail how demoralizing it is to live in a relationship marred by inconsistency and unreliability.

Conversely, when the people are 'faithful', God 'preserves'—protects, defends—them. The Psalms echo the praises of these 'faithful ones'.

Sometimes, many of us find ourselves deploring the weakness of our faith in God, viewed from the 'inside', as it were. When these feelings overtake us, the worst thing to do is to focus on the supposed weakness of our faith. Far better, surely, to turn our attention to the faithfulness of God. A weak faith in a strong God is obviously much better than a strong faith in a weak one!

A reflection

'I will proclaim the name of the Lord; ascribe greatness to our God! The Rock, his work is perfect, and all his ways are just. A faithful God, without deceit, just and upright is he' (Deuteronomy 32:3–4).

8

FORGIVENESS

To the Lord our God belong mercy and forgiveness, for we have rebelled against him, and have not obeyed the voice of the Lord our God by following his laws, which he set before us by his servants the prophets.

DANIEL 9:9–10

I remember leading a 'teaching mission' in a London church many years ago. We had a question-and-answer session at which an educated man, a medical doctor, asked me a question: 'What does the prayer mean when it says that God's "property is always to have mercy"?' At first I couldn't see his problem, then light dawned.

'Forget buildings,' I said. 'Think chemicals.'

I'm glad to say he got the point at once. Mercy is a 'property' of God in much the same way as reducing inflammation is a property of aspirin. In the light of this conversation, I was glad to see the wording changed in the new Common Prayer book of the Church of England to 'whose *nature* is always to have mercy'.

Mercy and forgiveness, as our passage of scripture says, 'belong' to God; they are his 'properties', part of his very nature. The God of the Bible, in both the Hebrew and Christian scriptures, is a God of forgiveness, which in essence means the re-establishment of a relationship after a rupture. He is a God of holiness, true, and the judge of all the earth, but above and beyond that he is a God who longs to heal and forgive those very things in human nature that damage our relationship with him.

However, in both Old and New Testaments, this forgiveness is never lightly awarded. In fact, it is always conditional. In order for forgiveness to take place, there must be repentance. The offender must confess the sin and genuinely renounce it. Without that element, forgiveness would be not only cheap, but virtually meaningless, because the damaged relationship would quickly be impaired once again.

We can see the principle vividly demonstrated in the story of David and Bathsheba (2 Samuel 11 and 12). The great king of Israel stayed in his palace while his army went off to confront an enemy. While idling on the palace roof, he saw from there a beautiful woman bathing. He enquired who she was and discovered she was the wife of one of the officers in his army, Uriah, who was, of course, away on military service. David brought her to his palace and, in the casual way of monarchs in those days, had intercourse with her. She became pregnant, and to cover up his sin David arranged for Uriah to be killed in battle, thus adding, in effect, murder to his adultery.

He thought he had got away with it, but 'the thing that David had done displeased the Lord' (11:27), who sent the prophet Nathan to confront him. Faced with his sin, David made no excuses: 'I have sinned against the Lord'. Nathan's response was equally succinct: 'Now the Lord has put away your sin; you shall not die' (12:13). The child who had been born to Bathsheba did die, however, despite David's praying to God and fasting that it might be spared.

Whatever we may make of the detail of the story, the one clear thing is that David's abject and immediate confession of his sin was the key to his forgiveness. This is the pattern all through the Old Testament—we can see it several times in the accounts of the wilderness journeys, where the children of Israel are forgiven many times when Moses, on their behalf, expresses repentance. It is, of course, equally strongly emphasized in the New Testament—we have only to think of the words of the Lord's Prayer: 'forgive us our sins, as we forgive those who sin against us'. Those who harbour an unforgiving spirit cannot themselves expect forgiveness.

In the Hebrew scriptures, the principle of sacrifices for sin carries the same message. Those who have sinned must acknowledge the fact and show, by the sacrifices they offer, that their repentance is real. One could think of this as a concrete or visible expression of repentance every bit as much as a 'payment' for sin. As we have already seen (under 'Atonement'), the whole system of sacrificial offerings was intended to underline the seriousness of sin—a truth which contemporary thought finds very uncongenial. Repentance is the inner truth behind the outward ritual, and without it, as the later prophets of Israel make clear, there can be no forgiveness (see, for example, Micah 6:6–8).

When the conditions are met, however, and real repentance has been demonstrated, the forgiveness of God is absolute and final. 'I, I am He who blots out your transgressions for my own sake, and I will not remember your sins' (Isaiah 43:25). What is so wonderful about that promise by God is that even the memory of our sins is erased from God's records. In human relationships, a common problem is that even faults that have been forgiven are not, in fact, forgotten, and can be brought up at painful moments in the future. With God, what is forgiven is forgotten.

A reflection

The story of the Prodigal Son (Luke 15:11–32) should really be called the story of the Forgiving Father. It is true that the son, sitting among the swine, finally comes to his senses and decides that he will get up and go to his father, and say to him, 'Father, I have sinned against heaven and before you'. And indeed, he did more than say it, he did it. But his father (whom any reader of the story will identify with our heavenly Father, God) was already on the lookout for such an event, and 'ran and put his arms around him'. There, in a form even a child can understand, is the ultimate picture of the God who forgives—indeed, 'whose nature is always to have mercy'.

9

GLORY

[Moses said] 'In the morning you shall see the glory of the Lord, because he has heard your complaining against the Lord...' Then Moses said to Aaron, 'Say to the whole congregation of the Israelites, "Draw near to the Lord, for he has heard your complaining."' And as Aaron spoke to the whole congregation of the Israelites, they looked toward the wilderness, and the glory of the Lord appeared in the cloud.

EXODUS 16:7, 9–10

In the year that King Uzziah died, I saw the Lord sitting on a throne, high and lofty; and the hem of his robe filled the temple. Seraphs were in attendance above him; each had six wings: with two they covered their faces, and with two they covered their feet, and with two they flew. And one called to another and said: 'Holy, holy, holy is the Lord of hosts; the whole earth is full of his glory.'

ISAIAH 6:1–3

Every valley shall be lifted up,
and every mountain and hill be made low;
the uneven ground shall become level,
and the rough places a plain.
Then the glory of the Lord shall be revealed,
and all people shall see it together,
for the mouth of the Lord has spoken.

ISAIAH 40:4–5

'Glory' is used so often in relation to God in the scriptures that it is obviously a fundamental expression of his nature and of how

38

human beings are to regard him. The Hebrew word (*kabod*) means 'weight' and so, by inference, 'power'. In the earlier biblical narratives, 'glory' is almost always connected with demonstrations of God's power in such phenomena as thunder and lightning. As the story unfolds, we see that these are simply expressions of more elusive qualities like sovereignty, holiness and justice. The God of the Hebrews is emphatically a God of power and might, as the intransigent Egyptians were to find out when he 'gained glory for [himself] over Pharaoh, his chariots, and his chariot drivers' (Exodus 14:18). He was not a puny, helpless idol, but a God of power and might.

In the first of our short passages, we see God's glory demonstrated to the rebellious, or at any rate whingeing, Israelites in the desert. They demanded food? He would rain food on them from heaven (Exodus 16:4)—but first they would have to understand the awesome source of this provision. What the precise nature of this 'glory' (v. 10) was we are not told—perhaps a dazzling sunset, or some unusual configuration of light and cloud in the sky. Whatever it was, it achieved its immediate purpose. The people believed, and waited; and at nightfall the flock of quail landed on their encampment, to provide them with tasty fresh meat for their evening meal. In the morning, the ground was covered with what they came to call 'manna', the food which sustained them all through the 40 years of the wilderness journey.

So here, 'glory' is the power of the Lord God, revealed in mighty acts of generosity. In our next passage 'glory' is a revealing or unveiling to the prophet of the awesome holiness and power of God. He is 'holy, holy, holy'—the *tersanctus*, the thrice holy, the ultimate touchstone of moral perfection. Isaiah's response is a common one in the face of utter purity and power: a recognition of his own sinfulness by comparison. Christians may compare it with Peter's reaction to the power of Jesus revealed in a miracle on the lake: 'Go away from me, Lord, for I am a sinful man' (Luke 5:8). It is a truth of spiritual growth that the nearer we draw to God and his glory, the more conscious we are of our own failures and sins. Glory has that effect on what is tawdry!

The third passage, from 'second' Isaiah (the later prophet who spoke of Israel's return from captivity), moves us on from a revelation of God's glory for his chosen people in the wilderness, or to his chosen prophet in the temple, to a day when his glory will be demonstrated to the whole world: 'all people' (v. 5). This will still occur, though, in the context of a revelation of mighty power, this time in the deliverance of his people from slavery and their return to the holy city of Jerusalem.

'Glory', all through the Hebrew scriptures, is inevitably associated with God's power. It is this, more than anything else, which distinguishes him from the gods of the heathen. The Lord God, Yahweh, is a God who actually does things, rather than just talking about them. Therefore, the glory which people offer to him is not empty worship of a meaningless idol, but a rational response to what he has done and is doing.

God's glory is often said to shine through a cloud, or to be represented by a cloud (see, for instance, Exodus 24:16–17). This may partly be to emphasize that it is only through a covering that human eyes can see such glory and live. Certainly, the Hebrew scriptures wish to emphasize that God's glory is not simply a remote phenomenon, but comes down among his people, most particularly, of course, in the tabernacle and later the temple. God's glory is to be seen both as transcendent—utterly other and above us—and immanent, close at hand, in our midst. This insight is invaluable when we turn to the New Testament. Indeed, it must be hard to understand the whole notion of 'glory', when applied to Jesus, without this Old Testament background.

There is another Hebrew word for glory, *shekinah*, which does not actually appear in the original Old Testament texts but only in other Jewish writings like the Targums (Aramaic versions of Old Testament writings) and rabbinic literature. It speaks of presence—God's presence among his people. In the Greek translation of the Old Testament, the Septuagint, this word seems to have influenced the translation of *kabod* by the Greek word *doxa* (brightness, splendour, power, holiness). It is then something of a shock to discover that in the New Testament *doxa*, the glory of God, is revealed in a human form, Jesus (John 1:14), and especially in his death on the cross (17:22).

A reflection

It is perhaps a surprise to find that human beings can 'glorify' God, indeed are constantly enjoined to do so (see, for instance, Psalm 22:23; 86:12). Obviously we can't somehow add to God's glory, but we can and should recognize it, submit to it and be grateful for it—and perhaps through our lives help others to recognize it. As the poet George Herbert says, 'In my heart, though not in heaven, I can raise thee'.

10

GRAVE (SHEOL)

For my soul is full of troubles,
and my life draws near to Sheol.
I am counted among those who go down to the Pit;
I am like those who have no help,
like those forsaken among the dead,
like the slain that lie in the grave,
like those whom you remember no more,
for they are cut off from your hand.
You have put me in the depths of the Pit,
in the regions dark and deep.

PSALM 88:3–6

If I ascend to heaven, you are there;
if I make my bed in Sheol, you are there.
If I take the wings of the morning
and settle at the farthest limits of the sea,
even there your hand shall lead me,
and your right hand shall hold me fast.
If I say, 'Surely the darkness shall cover me,
and the light around me become night,'
even the darkness is not dark to you;
the night is as bright as the day,
for darkness is as light to you.

PSALM 139:8–12

One of the temptations for the Christian studying the Hebrew
scriptures is to read back into them insights and beliefs which are
part of Christian tradition. Sometimes this is justified, especially

where one feels that there is a fulfilment of a prophecy. Where belief about death and resurrection is concerned, however, it can lead to a serious misreading of some of the books of the Old Testament, including many of the Psalms. It is generally agreed by biblical scholars that there is little evidence of belief in life beyond death—certainly not in the sense that later Judaism and hence Christianity believed it—in the formative first five books of the Bible, the Pentateuch. This was the basis of the denial by the Sadducees, in the time of Jesus, of the resurrection: their beliefs were strictly confined to those early books. Later additions to the scriptures were treated by them with suspicion.

It is true that Jesus argued that the formula 'the God of Abraham, the God of Isaac, and the God of Jacob', first found in Exodus (3:6), demonstrated that they were still 'alive', on the basis that God is not the 'God of the dead, but of the living' (Matthew 22:32), but it can safely be said that the people of patriarchal times would not have thought in those terms. When King David's little son died, after his affair with Bathsheba, David could only say: 'I shall go to him [that is, to the grave], but he will not return to me' (2 Samuel 12:23). Whatever Job meant by his great *cri de coeur*: 'I know that my Redeemer lives' (Job 19:25), biblical scholars would agree that this notoriously complicated piece of text cannot confidently be used to argue for a belief in physical resurrection that would seem to have been quite alien to Jewish thought at the time.

The Psalms are full of references to Sheol, often translated as the 'grave' or the 'Pit'—the abode of the dead. Sometimes the psalmist is full of gratitude because he has recovered from an illness which he had thought was going to consign him there (see, for instance, Psalm 6). The note of horror is stark: 'In death there is no remembrance of you; in Sheol who can give you praise?' (Psalm 6:5). Sometimes he is appalled at the fate of those who are already in Sheol, cut off from beauty, hope and even memory.

The picture would be of unrelenting gloom were it not for the element of hope and trust in God which pervades the Psalter. For the writers, even Sheol, the grave, is under the rule of the Lord God.

Indeed, Psalm 139 goes much further, as our second passage indicates: God is there, too! 'Even if I make my bed in Sheol, you are there' (v. 8)—in other words, those who sleep the sleep of death are still under God's protection and in his presence, which is not very far from the apostle Paul's insistence that the believing dead are 'with Christ', asleep, but only so that they may await the joyful resurrection (see 1 Corinthians 15:20–26).

In view of this element of trust and hope, even in the earliest parts of the scriptures, it isn't surprising that later Judaism formulated a belief in the resurrection of the just. Daniel is assured in a vision at the end of his book: 'But you, go your way, and rest; you shall rise for your reward at the end of the days' (12:13). We have, too, Ezekiel's vision of the dry bones that live (37:11–14). In some of the apocryphal books, a doctrine of resurrection is specifically spelt out: 'The souls of the righteous are in the hand of God… Their hope is of immortality' (Wisdom 3:1–3).

By the time of Christ we have the majority position, represented by the Pharisees and the beliefs of ordinary Jewish people like Martha (John 11:24), who believed in the resurrection of the dead, and the minority one, held by the Sadducees, who denied any belief in such a resurrection. Jesus, of course, was firmly with the majority view, for once, but took it a great deal further than the Pharisees with the claim: 'I am the resurrection and the life. Those who believe in me, even though they die, will live' (John 11:25).

However, belief in the resurrection should not close our eyes to the reality of Sheol, the grave, the Pit—*hades*, in New Testament language. Death, as we all know in our heart of hearts, is a cruel and necessary reality. It was to *hades*, the grave, that Jesus descended in order to proclaim the resurrection (certainly not to 'hell', as we used to say in the Creed).

The writers of those early books of the Bible and of the Psalms were deeply aware of the reality and finality of death, yet still clung to their faith in a God of hope. Christians rejoice in a faith that sees the grave itself as a gateway to eternal life. While doing that, can we also respect the people of God of an earlier era who believed and trusted in him while having no knowledge at all that any such reward awaited those who did so?

A reflection

'If I make my bed in Sheol, you are there'—what a thrilling expression of faith from the lips of a man who feared the grave more than his greatest mortal enemy. 'You are there', even in the place of dust and darkness. Indeed, there is nowhere in the whole of creation that is not under the just and gentle rule of Yahweh, the Lord God. Perhaps the last word might go to the risen Jesus, in John's vision: 'I was dead, and see, I am alive for ever and ever; and I have the keys of Death and of Hades' (Revelation 1:18).

II

HOLY

The Lord spoke to Moses, saying: 'Speak to all the congregation of the people of Israel and say to them: You shall be holy, for I the Lord your God am holy.'
LEVITICUS 19:1–2

'For I am the Lord your God; sanctify yourselves therefore, and be holy, for I am holy... For I am the Lord who brought you up from the land of Egypt, to be your God; you shall be holy, for I am holy.'
LEVITICUS 11:44a, 45

In these solemn words, one of the great themes of the Bible is laid down. God is holy. We are not. Since God can't become *less* holy in order to relate to humans, humans must become *more* holy to relate to him—a process the scriptures call 'sanctification'. 'You shall be holy', says the Lord to Moses—and Jesus echoed those very words in the Sermon on the Mount, 'Be perfect, therefore, as your heavenly Father is perfect' (Matthew 5:48). Unfortunately, for us it sounds like a command to attain the unattainable. Not only are we not 'holy', but within ourselves we seem to lack the capacity to attain to holiness.

The very word 'holy' is not one that appeals to ordinary people. 'Oh, don't be so *holy*', we say. Think of phrases like 'holy Joe' or 'holier than thou', and you can see how the word carries notions of piety and priggishness which we find deeply unattractive. Sadly, these ideas are built on a faulty understanding of what holiness is. We shall not get far in responding to God's call to holiness until we put that right.

God is holy. That was how this chapter started, but what does it mean to say that? 'Holy', in the biblical sense, means 'separate, different, untainted by fault'. Clearly, God is like that (or he wouldn't *be* God, if you see what I mean). People and things become holy only by connection with him, the source of holiness, rather than by some intrinsic or earned holiness of their own. The Bible speaks of holy people, of a holy nation (Exodus 19:6), and of holy objects, such as vestments, vessels and other objects. The ark of the Lord was 'holy'. The Hebrew scriptures also describe holy places and holy days. All of these things are only made holy by their association with God—in other respects, there is clearly no difference between one day and another, one nation and another, or one place on the map and another.

This principle of association or connection with God is an important one to keep in mind while considering the meaning of holiness. In our two short passages, for instance, the holiness which was required of the people of Israel is closely linked to their relationship to him. He brought them out of the land of Egypt and he is their God. That is the connection, the association. Without that link, they would be no different from every other tribe, and could certainly not be called a 'holy people'.

Just as God's holiness makes him separate or 'different', however, so does the holiness which comes from connection with him. As he is holy, so are his people. This doesn't mean that they can instantly attain a holiness similar to God's, but that they are called to holiness. Sanctification, in other words, is a *process* rather than a *crisis*. God's people are on the way to being made holy; it is their destiny and calling. At the same time, it doesn't automatically make them 'better' than the people of the surrounding nations who were not 'connected' to him. They have to do it to be it—all through the Bible, that is the reverse side of being God's people!

The story of the Old Testament is, sadly, the story of persistent failure to pursue the way of holiness, though Isaiah speaks of a day when a 'highway' shall run through the desert, a path for God's people leading to the holy city, Zion. This road is called the 'Holy Way', the way of holiness. Wonderfully, it is not just for the wise and the experienced spiritual pilgrim: 'no traveller, not even fools, shall go astray' (Isaiah 35:8). In other words, God will one day provide a pathway that will lead ordinary people, not just the super-pious, on to the place of holiness.

That underlines a profound scriptural truth. Because holiness is supremely an attribute of God, and of God alone, he is by definition the only source of holiness. Any pursuit of it apart from him is doomed to failure. The Hebrew scriptures are full of warnings about the vanity of religious rituals or observance which are not expressions of holy living. 'Will the Lord be pleased with thousands of rams?' asks Micah, 'with tens of thousands of rivers of oil?... He has told you, O mortal, what is good; and what does the Lord require of you but to do justice, and to love kindness, and to walk humbly with your God?' (Micah 6:7–8). It is hard to imagine a clearer definition of holiness than that, and it all depends, as Micah is at pains to point out, on maintaining that connection to the source of holiness himself, God. 'But as for me,' says the prophet, 'I will look to the Lord, I will wait for the God of my salvation; my God will hear me' (7:7).

A reflection

*It's obvious that there's no simple formula for becoming 'holy',
and no instant solution to the problem of human moral vulnerability.
But it's equally obvious that if the way to holiness is connection with
its source, God himself, then anything that draws us closer to him will
also draw us on to the 'way of holiness'. Prayer, scripture, sacrament,
worship—indeed, anything that creates time and space for God
in our lives—will be aids to our sanctification; and the neglect
of them will inevitably set it back.*

12

HOPE

> I wait for the Lord, my soul waits,
>   and in his word I hope;
>   my soul waits for the Lord
> more than those who watch for the morning,
> more than those who watch for the morning.
>   O Israel, hope in the Lord!
> For with the Lord there is steadfast love,
>   and with him is great power to redeem.
>
> PSALM 130:5–7

On the walls of the city there were watchmen whose task it was to look for the sunrise and then let the citizens know that a new day had dawned. That's the image which inspires this beautiful little piece of poetry. The watchmen did not doubt for a moment that sunrise would come, that morning would follow night, that the bright rays of dawn would drive away the shadows and light up the streets. They waited with confident hope, and that is what the psalmist celebrates.

When we use the word 'hope' in modern English, we often imply a degree of doubt, or at least wishful thinking. If you ask the plumber whether he can mend a leak, it's slightly discouraging if he replies, 'I hope so'. The implication is that there is some doubt, some hidden difficulty which may make it impossible. 'I hope so' often means not much more than an expression of a wish. In this way, 'hope' is evacuated of its true or original meaning. 'We can only hope', we say, as though that's a last resort.

The dictionary usually runs through a variety of meanings for the word, from 'expectation' through to 'probability' and then 'desire'.

A Hebrew dictionary would not recognize the last two definitions. Hope is an expectation, a deep-seated trust, a confidence in divine promises. It excludes, rather than embraces, doubt about the outcome. In short, it is a term which is central to the biblical world-view, a fundamental component of the life of the 'righteous'. Hope, in this understanding, is grounded in God and his promises. We can see in our passage that Israel was to hope 'in the word of the Lord' and then to 'hope in the Lord' himself. This would be a steadfast hope, not a pious wish. God keeps his promises (his word) and, as we have already seen, it is his very nature to be 'faithful', to keep faith with what he has promised. To hope in God is, if one can put it this way, to back a certainty.

In Old Testament thought, hope is closely allied to trust. Those who hope in the Lord trust him, and this gives them a general confidence in his protection and help (Jeremiah 29:11) and frees them from anxiety and fear (Psalm 46:2). In turn, this hopeful trust leads to the whole concept of 'waiting' for the Lord. If he has promised, then he will do it, even if the outcome is long delayed. In practice, he rewards those who patiently trust him by vindicating them—by bringing the justice for which they call: 'Commit your way to the Lord; trust in him, and he will act. He will make your vindication shine like the light, and the justice of your cause like the noonday. Be still before the Lord, and wait patiently for him' (Psalm 37:5–7a). There is a thought there for today's world, which wants everything now—'taking the waiting out of wanting', as the credit card slogan used to say.

Of course, there is misplaced hope. Hope that is not grounded in God and his promises is regarded as futile, particularly if it requires us to trust fallible human beings. This misguided hope can lead us into a totally false sense of security—'Shudder, you complacent ones' warns Isaiah (32:11). Riches can lead to false hope, and so can military might: 'The war horse is a vain hope for victory' (Psalm 33:17).

In the earlier books of the Hebrew scriptures, hope is most generally seen as temporal blessing from God—long life, many children, victory over enemies, land, cattle and so on. In later books, especially the Hebrew prophets, hope begins to look to the future, to the coming of the messianic kingdom and even the resurrection of the dead. It is this hope which is developed in the New Testament through the coming of Jesus, his death and resurrection and the promise of eternal life.

We have only to see what a cold word 'hopeless' is to recognize how central hope is to human life. Indeed, we say 'where there's life, there's hope'. The biblical world-view raises the notion of hope to a different level. To hope in God is to put our trust in the God of hope, with whom there is no defeat, no failure, no ending.

A reflection

'All my hope on God is founded; he doth still my trust renew'—Robert Bridges wrote the hymn that starts with those words; Herbert Howells wrote the music to it, and called it 'Michael' in memory of a very precious person who had died. In moments of human need and despair, hope in God and the fulfilment of his promises is marvellously healing. 'Why are you cast down, O my soul, and why are you disquieted within me? Hope in God; for I shall again praise him, my help and my God' (Psalm 42:5–6a).

13

IDOL

Then God spoke all these words: 'I am the Lord your God, who brought you out of the land of Egypt, out of the house of slavery; you shall have no other gods before me. You shall not make for yourself an idol, whether in the form of anything that is in heaven above, or that is on the earth beneath, or that is in the water under the earth. You shall not bow down to them or worship them.'

EXODUS 20:1–5a

There are no less than eleven different Hebrew words for 'idol' in the Bible, which shows how seriously the Jewish religion took them. Some simply mean 'statue', others 'household gods', 'image', 'figure', or, more crudely, 'detestable thing' or 'abomination'. From this it may be gathered that idols, however described or employed, were regarded as very bad things—at any rate, in theory, even if in practice household gods, for instance (known as *teraphim*), seem at times to be tolerated (see Genesis 31:19–55 and Judges 17:5, 7–13). These instances are mostly in the early history of Israel, it must be said. In general, and especially in the works of the great prophets of Israel, the denunciation and ridiculing of idol worship is fierce and uncompromising (see, for example, Isaiah 44:9–20).

This makes it all the more surprising that the Israelites themselves are time and again guilty of idolatry. In fact, the first public sin committed after the giving of the law to Moses was the making by the people—with Aaron's connivance—of a golden calf, which they worshipped and to which they offered sacrifices and said: 'These are your gods, O Israel, who brought you up out of the land of Egypt' (Exodus 32:8). It would be hard to imagine a more blatant act of idolatry than that, and it evoked from Moses absolute fury.

He broke the stone tablets bearing the Ten Commandments and ordered that the calf be melted, ground to powder and then drunk by the Israelites.

The first commandment, which is the passage at the head of this chapter—without its final warnings about God's 'jealousy' (in the sense of possessiveness, rather than envy)—sets out in peremptory terms the nature of idolatry. It is the worship of something of human devising in place of the worship of the one true God. These words defined for ever the heart of the faith of Israel: 'the Lord our God, the Lord is one' (Mark 12:29). Worshipping one God—monotheism, as it is called—distinguished the tribe of Israel from all the other tribes around them, with their multiplicity of gods. Not all were manufactured idols. Some worshipped the sun or the moon. The problem was the same in every case, however—the idols were themselves God's creatures, albeit in most cases re-shaped or moulded by human hands. It was the worship of the creature rather than the creator, of an object formed of the very substance which he had brought into being.

To say that the Israelites were not to have any god 'before' Yahweh, the Lord, is not at all to imply that other gods would be all right if they were 'after' him, regarded as secondary. That was the sin of the making of the golden calf. After all, when the people made their sacrifices to it they offered them 'to Yahweh, the Lord' (Exodus 32:5–6), but God was displeased. If there is only one creator God, one being worthy of human worship and praise, that worship can't, as it were, be delegated to some lesser divinity, especially one of human manufacture.

The danger for readers today is to see this commandment as irrelevant to us. It's true that there aren't a vast number of idols around us, in the form of physical objects of worship and devotion (as there were in Athens in Paul's day—Acts 17:16). But idolatry is alive and well and living in the modern world. Anything which takes the place which rightly belongs to God is idolatry. Sport, music, a hobby, success, the car, the investments, yes, even the garden—if they usurp the place in our lives that rightly belongs only to God, then they have become idols. They come 'before' him; they transfer our worship, praise, sense of what is valuable, away from God on to a siding. It may be a very pleasant siding, and in normal terms harmless and even laudable. Only the one who is there can know for sure whether that 'thing' has become a substitute god. A fairly simple way of checking is to ask ourselves what position that hobby, possession or commitment holds in our lives over against our commitment to God.

Idolatry, even in the Old Testament, took many strange forms. The divinely ordained brass snake with which Moses was able to counter a plague of the venomous beasts could, and did, become an object of idolatry (see and contrast Numbers 21:9 with 2 Kings 18:4). This should warn us about the dangers of devotional images which become ends in themselves, instead of means to an end, and that end the true worship of the one God.

A reflection

John's first letter, in the New Testament, ends rather abruptly: 'Little children, keep yourselves from idols' (1 John 5:21). This command makes better sense when read in conjunction with the previous sentence: 'He is the true God and eternal life' (1 John 5:20b). Idolatry is failure to recognize the true nature of God. He alone is to be worshipped.

14

INCENSE

I call upon you, O Lord;
come quickly to me;
give ear to my voice when I call to you.
Let my prayer be counted as incense before you,
and the lifting up of my hands as an evening sacrifice.

PSALM 141:1–2

Incense was widely used in the ancient world—indeed, long before the time of Abraham—for such things as funeral rites, other religious ceremonies, in the practice of magic and as a cosmetic. There is evidence of its use as far back as the fourth millennium BC. When it was adopted into Israelite religious practice, however, it was carefully regulated. The 'altar of incense' in the tabernacle (and later the temple) was to be the centre of the nation's intercession. Only priests were allowed to burn incense there, but it was seen by ordinary worshippers as signifying the lifting up of their own worship and prayer to God. So, in our passage, the psalmist can ask that his prayers should be 'counted' as incense before the Lord, just as his hands raised in worship were to be seen as part of the evening sacrifice offered by the priests.

Incense is, of course, created by burning aromatic herbs, such as frankincense, myrrh, aloes and balm. Although some, like frankincense, were acrid to the taste, they offered a sweet-smelling smoke when burnt. The practice of offering incense, though common in religious custom throughout the Middle East (including Egypt), was to become a specific part of the worship of the Jewish people. It was an ingredient, for instance, of the oil with which priests and kings were anointed (Exodus 30:34), it was to be burnt during the cereal offering (Leviticus 6:15) and the smoke which rose from the altar of incense was pleasing to God (Exodus 30:7). If it is not offered from a pure heart or with spiritual intent, though, the smell is offensive to him, indeed an 'abomination' (Isaiah 1:13). There is no magic about it. What matters in essence is the reality of the prayer, not the process of burning the incense.

That thought may help as we consider whether it is appropriate today for Christians to use incense in church or to burn it in their worship or private devotions. As so often in scripture, the answer lies not in the practice but in the intention. If the use of incense is an aid to prayer or worship, the equivalent of a visual aid—an odorous aid, perhaps?—then it's hard to see any objection. Incense is depicted in the imagery of the book of Revelation as representing the 'prayers of the saints' as they rise before God (Revelation 5:8), just as the sweet smell ascends from the incense burner. Some people will find that fanciful; others will find it a helpful and encouraging image.

On the other hand, if the burning of incense is in any way a substitute for true devotion, or offered to a false god, then instead of being helpful it becomes spiritually disastrous. 'I will punish her for the festival days of the Baals, when she offered incense to them', the Lord says to his unfaithful people (Hosea 2:13). Equally, sweet aromas will not placate a God whose righteousness has been offended. The incense may rise as far as the ceiling, but no further.

Incense suggests something of the inner beauty of true worship, the offering of our best and loveliest to God. Yet, as Jesus told the Samaritan woman at the well, 'true worshippers will worship the Father in spirit and truth' (John 4:23), rather than through carefully planned ceremonies in the 'right' place. Incense is the prayer of the heart lifted up to God. Without the heart, it is nothing.

A reflection

'Let my prayer be counted as incense before you':
that might make a fitting introduction to our evening devotions, the
longing that our thoughts and words may rise to the throne of God's
grace, unhindered by our unworthiness.

15

JOY

You show me the path of life.
In your presence there is fullness of joy;
in your right hand are pleasures for evermore.

PSALM 16:11

Those who think of the Old Testament as a rather grim book, featuring a God of judgment, a spot of ethnic cleansing and gallons of bloodshed, might be surprised to discover that one of the most common abstract nouns to be found in it is 'joy'. Some of this joy, it's true, is fairly manic—noisy celebrations of victories attributed to God's powerful right hand, sundry religious festivals and royal coronations. On such occasions, the noise must have been deafening and the excitement intense—for a taster, we could try Psalm 150:3–6! Indeed, the most common Hebrew word for joy comes from an Arabic source meaning 'excited'.

As the lovely verse from the Psalms which heads this chapter demonstrates, there is another kind of joy in its pages, too. This is the joy of faith, a joy which is a quality of life, not simply an emotional response, which is grounded and rooted in God himself —in fact, he is its source. This joy is most evident in the Psalter, where it is seen as the proper approach to worship, but also as an expression of personal adoration: 'O send out your light and your truth; let them lead me; let them bring me to your holy hill and to your dwelling. Then I will go to the altar of God, to God my exceeding joy; and I will praise you with the harp, O God, my God' (Psalm 43:3–4). There's no hint there of a fearful God of vengeance, only of a God who can truly be described as the psalmist's 'exceeding joy'.

In fact, joy just bursts out of the Psalms. The phrases flood through the pages. 'Glad with the joy of your presence', 'shout to God with loud songs of joy', 'the joy of all the earth', 'my lips will shout for joy', 'the trees of the forest sing for joy', 'the morning and the evening shout for joy'. If all this sounds, in the dismissive modern phrase, rather 'happy-clappy', then we could turn to Psalm 47:1: 'Clap your hands, all you peoples'. It would seem that the worship of the temple, while in its own terms solemn and awesome, was also exceedingly joyful—perhaps a lesson there for the Christian church today?

The great prophets of Israel also see joy as a natural expression of true salvation. More than the writers of the Psalms, perhaps, they are also aware that sin and disobedience are enemies of that joy. But they look on to a future restoration of Israel, a messianic golden age, and then, for sure, joy will fill the earth. Even the allegedly gloomy Jeremiah can promise such a future, when the one who scattered his people in judgment will gather them back to himself: 'Then shall the young women rejoice in the dance, and the young men and the old shall be merry. I will turn their mourning into joy, I will comfort them, and give them gladness for sorrow' (Jeremiah 31:13).

It is second Isaiah that brings together these two strands—the future hope, and the joy of a personal relationship with the creator. 'I will greatly rejoice in the Lord, my whole being shall exult in my God; for he has clothed me with the garments of salvation, he has covered me with the robe of righteousness, as a bridegroom decks himself with a garland, and as a bride adorns herself with her jewels. For as the earth brings forth its shoots, and as a garden causes what is sown in it to spring up, so the Lord God will cause righteousness and praise to spring up before all the nations' (Isaiah 61:10–11). The promise is of a future blessing, yet to be seen, but the prophet's experience is of a present joy, which does not spring from circumstances but from his 'whole being' rejoicing in God's salvation.

The people of Old Testament times lived, for the most part, hard lives. They worked hard, in the fields or raising the family; they were dependent on the harvest to feed them so that shortages and even famine were always a possibility, and their expectation of life, by our standards, was very short. They were often at the mercy of disease and epidemics, while war and enslavement were constant threats. Despite this, the genuine note of joy in so much of their religious worship must rebuke those of us who live in softer times, yet always seem more ready to blame God for our problems (even when largely self-inflicted) than to praise him for our blessings. The key, of course, is in an understanding that true joy is not simply a response to good things, but a quality which springs from true faith.

A reflection

'My whole being shall exult in my God.'

16

JUDGMENT

But the Lord sits enthroned forever,
he has established his throne for judgment.
He judges the world with righteousness;
he judges the peoples with equity.

PSALM 9:7–8

It's hard to understand the Hebrew scriptures without taking on board their profound belief in God as the judge of the whole earth. Right from the start, he is seen as the sole moral arbiter in his creation. In the story of the garden of Eden, he sets the rules, and he judges and punishes those who flout them. He judges the first act of homicide, by Cain, and fixes his sentence. He judges that human beings have become corrupted and destroys most of them in the flood, saving only Noah and his family, whom he has judged worthy of being saved. Whatever we wish to make of these early narratives, it is inescapable that the biblical authors want us to understand that this is not a creation without law or order and that God's creatures within it are not free to live amoral lives. All of them, whether they acknowledge him or not, live under his judgment. In the ringing words of Abraham, in an eloquent plea for justice, 'Shall not the Judge of all the earth do what is just?' (Genesis 18:25).

As the story continues, the unfolding picture is of a world under the judgment of God. That is not to be read as a sentence of guilt, but simply as a statement of truth. Our lives are lived under God's judgment. He alone, in the end, both sets the moral standards of the human race and judges us by our willingness to observe them. Being the sole judge, he also alone can exercise mercy and forgiveness: 'I… will show mercy on whom I will show mercy' (Exodus 33:19). This principle runs like a thread of steel all through the Old Testament, and much of it makes no sense at all if we ignore or evade it.

Because God's judgment is morally flawless, there is no appeal against it, though several delightful stories show great patriarchs like Abraham and Moses apparently doing precisely that (see, for instance, Genesis 18:23–33 and Exodus 32:7–14). Clearly, we are not meant to infer from these incidents that Abraham or Moses are either more just or more moral than God, so presumably the narrative is a dramatized way of showing how these great men of God endeavoured to understand the mind of the creator. God loves mercy; he is a God of forgiveness. There is abundant witness in the Hebrew scriptures to these divine qualities. He is also, as we have seen, a God of perfect holiness, who will not tolerate the corruption of his creation by evil in any form.

This tension is resolved, in part at least, by the power of any judge to commute a sentence ('I… will show mercy to whom I will show mercy') and by the provision for his people of a system of repentance, sacrifice and forgiveness by which his justice and his mercy can both be satisfied. None of this, of course, takes anything away from his absolute right of judgment, but from it we can deduce that the 'Judge of all the earth' is wise, compassionate and merciful. He has 'no pleasure in the death of anyone', but longs that the wicked shall turn away from their sin and find life (see Ezekiel 18:27, 32). In him, absolute justice and absolute love cohabit.

A reflection

Christians will see a further resolution of this tension, of course, in the Cross of Christ, where sin is both judged and forgiven—the place, as an old hymn says, 'where heaven's love and heaven's justice meet'.

17

KINGDOM

When your days are fulfilled and you lie down with your ancestors, I will raise up your offspring after you, who shall come forth from your body, and I will establish his kingdom. He shall build a house for my name, and I will establish the throne of his kingdom for ever. I will be a father to him, and he shall be a son to me. When he commits iniquity, I will punish him with a rod such as mortals use, with blows inflicted by human beings.
2 SAMUEL 7:12–14

These 'words of the Lord' were spoken by Nathan, the prophet of the Lord, to David in his old age. They could be said to establish the great Davidic dynasty, the kingdom of Israel which was to last for ever. David's son Solomon would build the great temple and (in this vision) the centuries would pass with the Lord's anointed, a descendant of David, seated on that throne, guiding God's people with justice, mercy and integrity.

That was the vision, but from the last days of Solomon onwards something went wrong. There were, it is true, good kings, like Uzziah, but there were also some notably bad ones. The tribes of Israel split between north and south, forming the two kingdoms of Israel and Judah. The people were several times taken off into captivity and exile, and eventually first the Greeks and then the Romans occupied and ruled the very lands that the Lord had designated for this chosen kingdom. That was, of course, the situation at the time of the birth of Jesus, a distant descendant of David and born in David's home town of Bethlehem.

Did that mean that God's purpose, as set out by Nathan, had been thwarted? The answer to that really depends on which of two balancing cases in the Hebrew scriptures we judge to be the most convincing. Scholars have always seen at least two literary influences at work in those scriptures, a 'priestly' hand and a monarchical one. Sometimes we seem to be seeing the history of Israel through one set of spectacles and at other times through another pair altogether. You can see the two influences at work in the rather tortuous account of the anointing of Israel's very first king, Saul, in 1 Samuel 8:4–22.

The people asked the prophet to give them a king, so that they could be like the nations around them. In doing that, the Lord responded, they would be rejecting his rule and seeking for another, human one—moving, in technical language, from a theocracy to a monarchy. Nevertheless, the elders pressed their case. They wanted a king to be their judge, their figurehead, their warrior-leader and their visible ruler. The Lord told Samuel to set out for the elders what a monarchy would involve: exploitation, bloodshed, injustice and greed. Yet still they persisted, and eventually (so the narrative goes) the Lord decided to let them have what they wanted, mainly, it would seem, to teach them a lesson. He instructed Samuel to appoint and anoint a king, and the choice fell on a Benjaminite, Saul.

For a while, Saul did well, winning notable victories over some of the local tribes. Later, however, certain weaknesses of temperament revealed themselves and 'the Lord rejected Saul from being king' (1 Samuel 16:1), specifically for failing to carry out the prophet's instructions where a victory over the Amalekites was concerned. Whether we are meant to see this as vindication of God's original reluctance to appoint a king at all—that is, as evidence that monarchy is at heart corrupt—or simply that Saul (rather like Judas Iscariot in the New Testament) failed to live up to his high calling, depends on which side of the continuing argument we choose to stand. The temple and priests were always rather suspicious of the kings; the kings were reluctant to have religious leaders interfering in matters of state. (We might feel that little changes with the passing of the centuries!)

Through all of this, and all the following centuries of struggle and disappointment, through bad kings and moderate kings and the occasional good king, the people of Israel and their prophets clung to the original vision. Sometimes imperfectly, sometimes clearly, they grasped the profound principle behind the idea of kingdom. There is, ultimately, only one 'king', and he is the Lord: 'the Lord is king for ever and ever' (Psalm 10:16). Therefore, all kingship devolves from him and to a certain extent mirrors his authority. A bad king is a kind of blasphemy, a distortion of the ideal. A good king, on the other hand, could give people a glimpse of the perfect rule of God that would one day encompass the whole earth.

Consequently, the great prophets saw Israel as a nation-state under God, and the Davidic kingship as the symbol of God's kingly rule exercised through a chosen and godly instrument. Increasingly, this vision merged into the larger messianic vision: there would come a time, perhaps long distant, when God would bring all his people together again, and restore the throne of David, which would bring blessing to the whole earth. There is a touch of the dream of a golden age about this, it is true, but as expressed by the great prophets of Israel, especially second Isaiah, it becomes a noble vision of a new way of living, possible only because it is within the will of God and promised by him.

So the people watched and waited and prayed through the centuries—waited for the restoration of the kingdom, a kingdom they would have thought of as the kingdom of David, but Christians, for sure, would identify with the kingdom of God.

A reflection

If God established a kingdom 'for ever', then clearly it cannot have a mortal as its ruler. What Nathan saw in his vision, and what we can see prefigured at times in the greater moments of the kingdoms of David and Solomon, was indeed a people living as a 'royal priesthood, a holy nation, God's own people' (1 Peter 2:9).

18

LOVE

From heaven he made you hear his voice to discipline you. On earth he showed you his great fire, while you heard his words coming out of the fire. And because he loved your ancestors, he chose their descendants after them. He brought you out of Egypt with his own presence, by his great power, driving out before you nations greater and mightier than yourselves, to bring you in, giving you their land for a possession, as it is still today. So acknowledge today and take to heart that the Lord is God in heaven above and on the earth beneath; there is no other. Keep his statutes and his commandments, which I am commanding you today for your own well-being and that of your descendants after you, so that you may long remain in the land that the Lord your God is giving you for all time.

DEUTERONOMY 4:36–40

You shall love the Lord your God with all your heart, and with all your soul, and with all your might.

DEUTERONOMY 6:5

I love the Lord, because he has heard my voice and my supplications.

PSALM 116:1

Moreover, the Lord your God will circumcise your heart and the heart of your descendants, so that you will love the Lord your God with all your heart and with all your soul, in order that you may live.

DEUTERONOMY 30:6

There is no single phrase from the Hebrew scriptures that can encompass the whole range of meanings and applications of the English word 'love'. Right from the start, however, the writers are clear that the primary love is that of God for his people: 'Because he loved your ancestors, he chose their descendants after them' (Deuteronomy 4:37). When Exodus sets out for the first time the Decalogue, the Ten Commandments, they are given as simple commands, requiring obedience. 'I am the Lord your God, who brought you out of the land of Egypt, out of the house of slavery; you shall have no other gods before me' (20:2–3). In Deuteronomy, the same law is spelt out, but introduced in terms of a response of love to God's generous acts: 'Hear, O Israel: The Lord is our God, the Lord alone. You shall love the Lord your God with all your heart, and with all your soul, and with all your might. Keep these words that I am commanding you today in your heart...' (6:4–6). The love which he expects—indeed, commands—from them is in response to his acts of love. He brought them out of the land of bondage; therefore they are under a debt of love. In the language of the New Testament, 'We love [him], because he first loved us' (1 John 4:19).

This love of God for his people is portrayed in Hosea as the love of a husband for his wife, even an unfaithful wife (3:1). His love is also seen as fatherly (Hosea 11:1–4) and even, by inference, that of a mother for her suckling infant (Isaiah 66:11). These illustrations mirror the love that characterizes human relationships at their best—Jacob's love for Rebekah, David's love for Jonathan (Genesis 24:67 and 2 Samuel 1:26). All human love, in other words, is a reflection of the love of the creator, who is its source and origin—again, in New Testament language, 'God is love' (1 John 4:16).

The passages of scripture above tell the story of the relationship of God's love to ours. It begins with God's act of grace in choosing a people: not because they particularly deserved it, but as an act of love. 'Because he loved... he chose'. As an act of response to that unmerited love, we are called to keep his commandments—again, not on some divine whim, and not out of servile fear, but simply because we wish to please the one we love. The psalmist expresses that love as a further response to daily blessings: 'I love the Lord, *because…*' The passage from Deuteronomy is a reminder that love flows not from cold logic, nor from an act of will, but from the heart. God will 'circumcise' the hearts of his people, set them free, remove all hindrance, so that they may love him completely.

There is a further word in the Old Testament which is sometimes translated 'love', but usually with an addition: 'loving-kindness', 'steadfast love', 'faithful love'. These are translations of the Hebrew word *chesed*, which describes the perfect love of God. Its primary quality is its unchanging nature (it is 'steadfast', 'faithful')—unlike much human love, which tends to be fickle and to change with our changing moods and feelings. God's love, like his very nature, is unchanging, totally reliable. 'The steadfast love of the Lord is from everlasting to everlasting' (Psalm 103:17a). 'I have loved you with an everlasting love' (Jeremiah 31:3). There is something very reassuring about a love like that.

Chesed also conveys a notion of gentleness. That is what makes the King James Version's 'loving-kindness' such a satisfying concept. God's love for his people, even when they are rebellious or disobedient, is marked by a love which is 'kind'. His faithfulness, in other words, is not a reluctant by-product of his nature but at the very heart of it.

A reflection

'Loved with everlasting love, led by grace that love to know.'
GEORGE WADE ROBINSON (1838–77)

19

MAKER

Know that the Lord is God.
It is he that made us, and we are his;
we are his people, and the sheep of his pasture.

PSALM 100:3

The whole of the Hebrew scriptures are based on its opening statement: 'In the beginning... God created the heavens and the earth' (Genesis 1:1). God made us, and everything that exists. He is, as the Creed puts it, the creator of 'all things, visible and invisible'. The first and most fundamental thing for a human being to know is that stark fact. He is our creator, and we are his creatures. As our verse says, 'he made us... and we are his; we are his people, and the sheep of his pasture'.

In one important sense, that determines our relationship with God. Because he made us, he has rights over us, just as the maker of a chair or a table can be said to own it. The Bible makes it clear, however, that we are more, much more, than simply objects made for his pleasure or gratification. We are not only made, but made in his image (Genesis 1:26). That doesn't mean, of course, that we look like him, or are in any physical sense copies of the divine—such ideas are the product of a kind of reversed thinking, in which God is visualized in our image, ideas which are described as 'anthropomorphic' and speak of God's hands or feet or heart. God is spirit (as Jesus asserted in John 4:24), not flesh and blood. The Thirty-Nine Articles of the Church of England put it very bluntly: 'There is but one living and true God, everlasting, without body, parts or passions'. We are made in his image and must resist the temptation to make him in ours!

Because God made us, we are his, not as objects but as 'children'. We are possessed by him in the sense that the sheep are 'possessed' by the shepherd: we are in his care, under his hand, dependent on his protection. Older versions of Psalm 100 include a small but telling extra clause to the verse quoted above: 'It is he that hath made us, and not we ourselves' (KJV). Our very existence is not self-willed, but God-willed. This is not just a matter of abstract theology, but should affect very deeply the way we relate to God. Because God is our creator, because we live in a creation rather than in an environment which is the product of an accident or the result of chemical or cosmic processes, we relate to it not simply with curiosity, questions and scientific analysis, but with awe. Whatever the means by which our universe and life itself came into existence, ultimately it was by the will of God. What we see and experience is the visible evidence of his power, wisdom and beauty, and we live our lives not as aliens on a strange planet but as children in the parental home. It really does make a difference to the way that we live and the way we treat our environment.

It is also worth looking at the difference in English between two words, 'maker' and 'creator', both of which are used to translate the same idea in the Bible. Strictly speaking, a maker takes existing material and fashions it into something new. The maker of a chair takes wood, glue and possibly nails or screws and with those materials brings into being something that previously only existed under those different forms. What was previously wood, glue and nails is now something we can identify as a chair. We can also recognize its maker.

If we speak of a 'creator', however, we usually mean someone who brings into being something which previously didn't exist at all. For instance, there was a time when Beethoven's seventh symphony didn't exist. There were only six of them! But then the composer sat down at his piano and began to translate sounds and ideas into notes on a page of manuscript, until eventually the whole work existed and could be performed by an orchestra. When we hear its magnificent sounds today, it's worth remembering that there was a time when it didn't exist and that when it came into existence it was entirely the product of Beethoven's mind and imagination. It was 'his' in a sense that a physical object could never be, because it was not a re-shaping of what already existed but solely the product of his own genius.

In much the same way, it is probably more helpful to speak in English of God as our creator rather than simply our maker. Before the creation there was 'only' God; after it—and solely as the product of his mind, imagination and genius—there was, in nucleus at least, the material universe, replete with the promise of life itself. Through the 'word' of God—'Let there be light'— something which hitherto had no existence sprang into being. Like Beethoven's seventh symphony, it owed its existence entirely to the genius of its creator.

A reflection

It seems inconsistent, to say the least, to speak of God as creator and then treat his creation with indifference or even contempt. Those who know that the 'Lord is God', and recognize that 'he made us and we are his', surely cannot treat the earth's human or animal residents with anything less than respect, nor set out to exploit selfishly the earth's resources as though they were ours, and not his.

MANNA

The Lord spoke to Moses and said, 'I have heard the complaining of the Israelites; say to them, "At twilight you shall eat meat, and in the morning you shall have your fill of bread; then you shall know that I am the Lord your God."' In the evening quails came up and covered the camp; and in the morning there was a layer of dew around the camp. When the layer of dew lifted, there on the surface of the wilderness was a fine flaky substance, as fine as frost on the ground. When the Israelites saw it, they said to one another, 'What is it?' For they did not know what it was. Moses said to them, 'It is the bread that the Lord has given you to eat…' The house of Israel called it manna; it was like coriander seed, white, and the taste of it was like wafers made with honey. Moses said, 'This is what the Lord has commanded: "Let an omer of it be kept throughout your generations, in order that they may see the food with which I fed you in the wilderness, when I brought you out of the land of Egypt."'

EXODUS 16:11–15, 31–32

'Manna' was the basic food of the Israelites on their long journey from Egypt to the Promised Land under the leadership of Moses. As we read here, it was found on the ground each morning (with the remarkable exception of the morning of the sabbath, when it didn't appear). It was, we are told, wafer-like, possibly farinaceous, sweet and tasty with a flavour of coriander and honey. Not bad for emergency fare on the journey!

It was given by God. About that, the scriptures are very clear. With this food, the Lord would provide for his people as they made their slow progress through desert and hill country. It was supplemented, at least on its initial appearance, with some fresh poultry, thanks to the timely arrival of an exhausted flock of quail over the camp. Normally, however, this 'manna' was their diet, to be seen as a gift of God to his people and as a means of teaching them to depend on him whatever the circumstances. As a lasting demonstration of their gratitude, Moses ordered that a quantity of it should be put in a jar and kept in the tabernacle, right at the heart of the worship of Israel.

The word itself is interesting. When the people saw it, they said to one another, 'What is it?'—*man hu* in Hebrew—and that became its name. It earths the whole experience to find that this priceless, life-saving gift of God was known to the Israelites as 'Wotsit', because that is literally what its name means.

Anyway, manna (or wotsit) was to be their staple diet for the next forty years or so. Its presence was a daily reminder that their journey was being undertaken at God's command and under his control. The fact that God fed his people on their pilgrimage was to become a foundation truth of the faith of Israel, constantly referred to by the psalmist, of course. It is also a truth reflected in the Lord's Prayer, 'Give us this day our daily bread', or, more precisely, our 'bread for the day'. It is also part of the imagery of the Christian eucharist, often described as 'pilgrim food'. Christians will remember how Jesus drew an exact parallel between the gift of manna and the gift of himself, the 'bread of life' (see John 6:32–35, 48–51).

Not surprisingly, there have been many attempts to find rational parallels for manna, and indeed botanists and nutritionists have tried to identify it with various substances that occur naturally in desert regions—notably secretions from plants or insects, some of which apparently do carry the kind of flavours described in the book of Exodus. However, while it may well be that the presence of manna from time to time could be rationally explained, it is very hard to fit such explanations into the narrative of a 40-year journey, especially when supplies didn't arrive on the sabbath! The implication is that, whatever the historical facts of the case, so far as the writer was concerned (and undoubtedly Moses and his companions, too) this was a miraculous provision by God, which made possible what would surely otherwise have been impossible —the journey of a large tribe of many thousands of people across what was undeniably hostile, barren and unproductive terrain.

Led and fed by God, the moaning mass moved slowly across the deserts of Sinai. There were moments of joy, of course, as well as times of doubt and near rebellion. More than any other single factor, this strange food, God's 'wotsit', made the journey possible. Over the years, the people of Israel forgot many things, but I think it's fair to say they never forgot that, as anyone who has attended a Jewish Passover meal will know!

A reflection

Thus they march, the pillar leading,
light by night and shade by day;
daily on the manna feeding,
which he gives them when they pray.
JOHN NEWTON (1725–1807)

21

MERCY

The Lord is gracious and merciful,
slow to anger and abounding in steadfast love.
The Lord is good to all,
and his compassion is over all
that he has made.

PSALM 145:8–9

'Mercy' is a characteristic of the God of the Bible, and that is as true of the picture of him which we have in the Old Testament as it is in the New. He is good; he is holy; he is just… and he is 'full of mercy'. That mercy is shown in many ways, but is always seen as part of his very character. The people of Israel would quickly learn that this did not by any means mean that he was 'soft', turning a blind eye to their sins, but rather that he was always ready to have mercy on those who acknowledged their faults and turned back to him.

All of that is common knowledge to anyone who has read much of the Hebrew Bible. However, any consideration of the meaning of the words 'mercy' or 'merciful' as they occur in its pages is complicated by the fact that from time to time they translate several different Hebrew words which express very different concepts. For instance, we have already dealt with one of those concepts in a previous chapter, on 'Love', because the word *hesed*, which speaks of the faithful love of God, is often also translated by 'mercy' or 'merciful', as well as by 'kindness' and its extended form, 'loving-kindness'. This notion of faithfulness is important to our under-standing of the idea of a God of mercy, because it roots God's mercy in his covenant love for his people, and is consequently not based on whim or mood (or even righteous indignation) but on his 'steadfast love'. As N.H. Snaith puts it in his book *The Distinctive Ideas of the Old Testament*, 'This steady, persistent refusal of God to wash his hands of wayward Israel is the essential meaning of the Hebrew word.' God's mercy is reliable and not dependent on human deserving. As the Lord said to Moses, when he had pleaded for the people's forgiveness after they had made the golden calf, 'I will be gracious to whom I will be gracious, and will show mercy on whom I will show mercy' (Exodus 33:19). In other words, God does not need to justify his acts of mercy or provide reasons for them. They are simply expressions of his nature.

Another Hebrew word sometimes translated by 'mercy' is *hanan*, which also means 'merciful' and 'gracious'. This speaks of God's mercy as an undeserved gift, the gracious favour of the superior to the inferior. It emphasizes that God's mercy cannot be earned, only granted.

A third Hebrew word which is sometimes translated by 'mercy' is *raham*, which more commonly expresses the idea of brotherly or maternal feeling. It also appears in the Old Testament as 'compassion', or, in its plural form, 'tender mercies'. As Karl Barth said of this word, 'The Personal God has a heart'. God's mercy flows from his love.

As can be seen, all three of these ideas are present in our passage. The Lord is 'gracious and merciful', he abounds in 'steadfast love' and in his kindness his 'compassion is over all'. In any approach to biblical language, it is always wise to unify ideas rather than dissect them, so it may be enough to say that the God of the Bible is, quite simply, a God of mercy based on faithful love.

Even a cursory reading of the Old Testament will, of course, demonstrate that God's mercy needs to be held in balance in our thinking with his justice and holiness. To say that God is merciful is not at all the same as to say that God is *only* merciful, just as to say that God is love is not to imply that he is not anything else. In the character of God these elements are not mutually exclusive but exist, it would seem, in a kind of creative tension. As Moses and the

Israelites learnt on their wilderness journey, it was dangerous to presume on God's mercy, but it was also foolish to leave it out of the reckoning.

A reflection

God of mercy, God of grace
Show the brightness of thy face…
HENRY FRANCIS LYTE (1793–1847).

22

OFFERING

When you present a grain-offering baked in the oven, it shall be of choice flour: unleavened cakes mixed with oil, or unleavened wafers spread with oil. If your offering is grain prepared on a griddle, it shall be of choice flour mixed with oil, unleavened; break it in pieces, and pour oil on it; it is a grain-offering. If your offering is grain prepared in a pan, it shall be made of choice flour in oil. You shall bring to the Lord the grain-offering that is prepared in any of these ways; and when it is presented to the priest, he shall take it to the altar. The priest shall remove from the grain-offering its token portion and turn this into smoke on the altar, an offering by fire of pleasing odour to the Lord. And what is left of the grain-offering shall be for Aaron and his sons; it is a most holy part of the offerings by fire to the Lord.

LEVITICUS 2:4–10

'When do we bring up the offering?' the churchwarden asked me rather anxiously. After all, I was the visiting minister, and he didn't want chaos and confusion at a critical point in the service. That's just about the only time I hear the word 'offering' nowadays—the slightly awkward process in church which others call (probably more truthfully) the 'collection', when bags or plates are passed around the congregation for gifts of money to be put in them. I can imagine what my churchwarden would have felt if someone had a sweet little lamb or a pair of doves to 'offer' at that point of the proceedings. In ancient Israel, monetary offerings were not a usual part of worship, though they became so in later centuries, of course—there is the story in the Gospels of the poor widow who put her very last coins into the temple treasury (Luke 21:1–4).

At the heart of the worship of the temple—which means, at the heart of the worship of Israel—was a vast and complex system of offerings and sacrifices. Indeed, the receiving of them by priests at the altar was the chief business of the temple. Day after day, week after week, thousands of people would enter its courts, bringing with them sheep, goats, calves, fruit and grain. Many were offered for sacrifice (which we shall consider in a later chapter), but some were principally offerings, gifts to God, expressions of gratitude or devotion, sometimes spontaneous and sometimes because they were decreed by law. In our passage, we have a description of one particular kind of offering, a 'grain-offering', with detailed instructions as to how it was to be offered by the worshipper and received by the priest.

To appreciate the practice of offerings, it is necessary to remember that the temple was seen as the place where the Lord God had his dwelling. That's not to say that the people of Israel thought that God could be contained in a building, however vast and impressive. At the consecration of the temple, King Solomon made that absolutely clear: 'Even heaven and the highest heaven cannot contain you, much less this house that I have built!' (1 Kings 8:27). His answer to the dilemma was to pray that God's 'name' (v. 29) would be there, and that from heaven, his 'dwelling-place' (v. 30), he would regard the prayers and offerings of the people made there. In practice, of course, popular understanding is seldom as subtle as that, and the temple was generally and acceptably thought of as 'the house of God'.

So it was there that offerings and sacrifices were made. The sacrifices were usually for sin, the offerings were of duty or gratitude (or both). Because sacrifices and offerings were made to God, rather than to any human person or institution, they were ceremonially burnt on the altar, the smoke carrying the gift to heaven—indeed, the odour of the burnt-offering was often described as 'pleasing to God' (Leviticus 8:21). In reality, the stench of blood and burning flesh must have made the altar area of the temple thoroughly unpleasant.

The kind of offerings described here were some of many

prescribed in Leviticus, which is effectively the manual of temple ritual. Some were first-fruits from harvest; some were to mark special occasions or festivals. They included drink offerings of wine, elevation (or 'wave') offerings, freewill-offerings, guilt-offerings, and what Leviticus rather beautifully describes as 'offering[s] of well-being' (7:11). In the particular case of the grain-offering described, a small part of the offering was burnt on the altar, the remainder being available for the priests. From such offerings, the priesthood was supported and the running costs of the temple were met. Money did not become the normal vehicle of business or payments until later, but when it did, a temple tax was instituted, and also a treasury, in which monetary gifts could be placed. Both of these feature in the New Testament, of course (Matthew 17:24; Mark 12:43).

It is a mark of humanity, it would seem, to offer gifts as acts of affection or gratitude. In fact we all do it—Christmas, birthdays, anniversaries, or simply to show our appreciation of someone. The temple offerings were ritualized ways for the people of Israel to show their love and gratitude for God. Doubtless, they were often given for wrong motives, or under the misguided impression that the donor could somehow gain the favour or help of the deity, yet at their best they must have represented costly expressions of devotion. Nevertheless, on several occasions the Hebrew scriptures make it clear that more important than our gifts of grain or animal sacrifice is the devotion of a true heart. David's penitential psalm makes the point eloquently: 'For you have no delight in sacrifice; if I were to give a burnt-offering, you would not be pleased. The sacrifice acceptable to God is a broken spirit; a broken and contrite heart, O God, you will not despise. Do good to Zion in your good pleasure; rebuild the walls of Jerusalem, then you will delight in right sacrifices, in burnt-offerings and whole burnt-offerings; then bulls will be offered on your altar' (Psalm 51:16–19). It's worth noticing that the psalmist is not condemning root and branch the offering of sacrifices, only their offering from hearts that are not 'broken and contrite'. When the heart is right, so is the offering, as Jesus made clear in the Sermon on the Mount (Matthew 5:23, 24).

A reflection

'What shall I return to the Lord for all his bounty to me?
I will lift up the cup of salvation, and call on the name of the Lord'
(Psalm 116:12–13).

23

PASSOVER

Then Moses called all the elders of Israel and said to them, 'Go, select lambs for your families, and slaughter the passover lamb. Take a bunch of hyssop, dip it in the blood that is in the basin, and touch the lintel and the two doorposts with the blood in the basin. None of you shall go outside the door of your house until morning. For the Lord will pass through to strike down the Egyptians; when he sees the blood on the lintel and on the two doorposts, the Lord will pass over that door and will not allow the destroyer to enter your houses to strike you down. You shall observe this rite as a perpetual ordinance for you and your children. When you come to the land that the Lord will give you, as he has promised, you shall keep this observance. And when your children ask you, "What do you mean by this observance?" you shall say, "It is the passover sacrifice to the Lord, for he passed over the houses of the Israelites in Egypt, when he struck down the Egyptians but spared our houses."' And the people bowed down and worshipped.

EXODUS 12:21–27

The story of Passover is one that runs like a thread through the history of the Jewish people, from the event described here, a full millennium before Christ, to the ceremony observed today in Jewish homes all over the world every April. During that time, like most rituals, it has undergone a number of changes and modifications, but it still retains its central features: a common meal, unleavened bread (*matzos*), the recitation of the story of the last plague and the release from Egypt, and the command to continue the tradition for ever.

Once the Israelites had settled in their own land, the Passover was celebrated centrally (eventually, of course, in the temple) as well as in individual homes. People would bring an animal (a young lamb, or, it would seem, a goat), which would be killed by the priest and its blood sprinkled on the altar. The people would eat the roasted meat (though some traditions say it was boiled) accompanied by the unleavened bread and various bitter herbs. By the time of Jesus the ritual had become more complex, with the addition of various cups of wine—four in all—at various stages of the meal.

After the destruction of the temple and the dispersion of most of the Jewish people, Passover became a home-based occasion, which it remains to this day. The only exception is the Samaritan Passover, which is still celebrated on the slopes of Mount Gerizim, and probably preserves some of the original features which have been lost in the passage of time.

Wherever it is celebrated, Passover fulfils the same function for the Jewish people. It is the recitation of their own unique story and an act of collective thanksgiving for the event which created a nation from a wandering tribe. Rather like Christmas in Christian cultures, Passover is observed even by those who are not seriously practising Jews the rest of the year, and by some who may even doubt the reliability of the history on which it is based. It is their story, and its recitation year by year has engraved it on the collective memory.

As far as that historical event is concerned, the basic narrative is clear enough. Pharaoh had resisted the various plagues which had afflicted Egypt, obstinately refusing to allow the Israelites to leave, even on a temporary permit—probably because he had a shrewd suspicion that they would never come back. Now the last and deadliest plague was threatened, the death of the first-born sons of Egypt. In order to spare the Hebrew children, their families were instructed by Moses to kill a young lamb and to daub its blood on the doorposts of their houses. When the angel of the Lord saw the blood, he would 'pass over' them—*pesach*, in Hebrew, which gave the ritual the name 'Passover'. Having killed the lamb, they were to eat it 'in haste', dressed ready for a journey, their 'loins girded'—their clothing hitched up at the waist (Exodus 12:11). There would be no time for bread to rise, so they were to bake it without yeast, which is the origin of the unleavened bread eaten by Jews at Passover. The notion of yeast as representing a source of moral pollution seems to have been a later development.

During the night, the awful calamity fell upon the land, with the death of the first-born males, from the son of Pharaoh to the sons of slaves and prisoners. The children of the Hebrews, however, were spared the fate; the Passover ritual had achieved its purpose. Urged on by the Egyptians, who were now anxious that they should depart, the Hebrews left the land for ever, making their way eastwards towards the Red (or probably Reed) Sea. Needless to say, that awesome night would live in the memories of those who had experienced it, but to ensure that it was never forgotten, Moses, at the Lord's command, gave instructions that the story was to be retold at the same time each year for ever. Today, all over the world, wherever Jewish people live, families gather for an annual meal (the *seder*), at which a child asks the question 'What do you mean by this observance?' and then the whole narrative is recited and the original meal re-enacted. In fact, the modern observance is different in a number of ways—over the years, various other bits of custom and tradition have got added to it—but the central element, the retelling of the story, remains. If the covenant with Abraham is the theological foundation of Judaism, the story of the Passover provides its corporate identity. Modern-day Jews do not say in the ceremony that their 'ancestors' were brought out of Egypt, but that *they* were: 'You brought us out of slavery'. The Passover takes history and applies it to the present, or rather it makes what happened once at a distant date in the past real and actual now.

A reflection

For Christians it is, of course, deeply significant that it was at the Passover that Jesus adapted the ancient ceremony to institute another ordinance for God's new people to observe for ever: the Lord's supper, the eucharist. In that ritual they, too, take an event from the distant past, the death on the cross of the Lord Jesus, and make it real and actual now.

24

PEOPLE

And I will have pity on Lo-ruhamah, and I will say to Lo-ammi, 'You are my people'; and he shall say, 'You are my God.'
HOSEA 2:23b

This rather obscure verse actually sums up with remarkable brevity the Old Testament doctrine of the 'people of God', a phrase which occurs over and over again in its pages. 'Lo-ruhamah' means 'not pitied' and 'Lo-ammi' 'not my people', and they were the names of the two children whom the unfaithful wife Gomer bore to the prophet Hosea, a daughter and a son. It would seem that in some way they represented the people of Israel, who, like Gomer, had been unfaithful, but to the Lord rather than to a human husband.

Because of their unfaithfulness and disobedience, the people of Israel had forfeited God's pity and protection, and consequently endured a period of intense suffering. From this, however, they would eventually turn, won back to God by his tender words and gentle persuasion. In the light of this repentance ('she shall respond as in the days of her youth'—Hosea 2:15) God would be able to restore them, so that Lo-ruhamah, the one who had forfeited pity, would now again be the object of his pity, and Lo-ammi, the one who was not his people, would be given back that title. The latter transaction is effectively summed up in two short phrases: 'You are my people' and 'You are my God'. And that, in a nutshell, is what it means to be the people of God.

There are, of course, other 'people' in the Hebrew Bible, notably the Gentiles (goy) and any nation or ethnic group (l'ummim). It would be wrong to think that they were regarded by God as any less significant than the so-called 'chosen people' of Israel. It was simply that he had a different purpose for them and was working in their case to a different timetable. His love encompassed all people without distinction or preference, but in order to bless the whole human race he chose to work through one small part of it.

So a third word for people, *am*, came to be applied almost exclusively to Israel as God's 'people', the people through whom that blessing was to come. This meaning of the word was acquired rather than intrinsic—its Greek equivalent in the scriptures is *laos*, which is the root of the English word 'laity', 'people'. However, in its acquired meaning, it referred to the chosen people, those called by God and in a covenant relationship with him.

As we have seen, this covenant was of grace and law, in the sense that God sought out the children of Israel and called them, making a covenant of promise with Abraham, the father of the tribe, but later supplemented it with the law, which would be a measure of the extent to which the people, from their side, were keeping the covenant. Their consistent failure to do so meant that frequently in the history of the twelve tribes of Israel and Judah they effectively ceased to be 'his people', though his love for them never faltered. As we see in the book of Hosea, however, as soon as they turned back to him, those who had forfeited pity and ceased to belong were welcomed back as beloved children.

At the heart of the whole notion of being 'the people of God' is this double responsibility. His people depend on him; he cares for them. He makes them his own cherished possession; they acknowledge him as their God and Father.

A reflection

The apostle Peter describes the Church in very similar terms to these.
Christians are 'chosen and destined by God the Father and sanctified by
the Spirit to be obedient to Jesus Christ and to be sprinkled with his
blood' (1 Peter 1:2a). Not only that, but they are a 'chosen race, a royal
priesthood, a holy nation, God's own people' (2:9a). The echoes of the

original covenant are unmistakable. There is still a 'double responsibility'. Like the people of God of old, we depend on him; he cares for us. He makes us his own cherished possession; we acknowledge him as our God and Father.

25

PRAISE

For great is the Lord, and greatly to be praised;
he is to be revered above all gods.
For all the gods of the peoples are idols,
but the Lord made the heavens.
Honour and majesty are before him;
strength and beauty are in his sanctuary.
Ascribe to the Lord, O families of the peoples,
ascribe to the Lord glory and strength.
Ascribe to the Lord the glory due his name;
bring an offering, and come into his courts.
Worship the Lord in holy splendour;
tremble before him, all the earth.

PSALM 96:4–9

'Serenading God' was how one cynic described it, and I remember myself, as a young choirboy, wondering whether even God might sometimes get as bored as we did at constantly hearing the same words and songs of praise. Why, we might ask, does an omniscient God need to be told over and over again how wonderful he is?

The answer, such as it is, goes to the heart of what praise meant to the people of Israel, and still means to the Christian Church. Our praise of God is not intended to tell him something he doesn't already know, or hasn't heard ten thousand times before, but to express how we feel about him. As the besotted lover gazes into the eyes of the beloved and says, 'Darling, you are beautiful!' he isn't making a cool analysis of the shape of her cheek-bones or the sweep of her eyelashes. He is not describing how she is, but how he regards her. That is, in fact, praise and worship rolled into one.

Worship is second nature to human beings, and expressing it is one of the greatest experiences we can have. If a football team is worthy of worship—look at the faces; hear the chants and the songs; see the banners—and, at the other end of the cultural ladder, if Shakespeare's sonnets can make transitory human love sound like an immortal property, then praise and worship of a creator God seems entirely justified.

Three words are widely used in the Hebrew scriptures to convey the idea of praise. *Halal* is basically about making a noise ('Make a joyful noise to the Lord...'—Psalm 100:1); *yada* is associated with bodily actions and ceremonial acts ('bow down... kneel before the Lord'—Psalm 95:6) and *zamar* is connected with music and singing ('praise him with the lute and harp'—Psalm 150:3b). In these ways, the worshipper's voice, mind and body all combine to offer praise to God. The whole of the Old Testament is saturated with such outbursts of praise and worship, some arising spontaneously from a feeling of gratitude, some in wonder and awe at God's mighty acts in creation and some—perhaps praise in its purest form—simply arising from sheer joy in his presence. None of these seems to have the slightest connection with a young choirboy's boredom! As C.S. Lewis put it, 'In commanding us to glorify him, God is inviting us to enjoy him' (*Reflections on the Psalms*, 1958, p. 95).

Praise is meant to be enjoyed. That may come as a surprise to the millions of people in Western Europe who regard church as 'boring'. The truly sad thing is that their opinion is often born of a youthful experience of church worship, which seemed to them, and probably was, far removed from the joyful explosion of delight that characterizes worship in the Bible, and surely ought to characterize it in our churches. Far from offering praise with the noise of our voices, we try to rein them back to a polite mutter. Far from our bodies being released to express awe and wonder, we tend to stand in a rigid pose, as though afraid to flex a muscle in such solemn circumstances. Far from the banging of tambourines and the clashing of cymbals, such praise is labelled 'happy-clappy' (even though Psalm 47 commands us to clap our hands together). I am no great fan of dancing in the aisles, I confess—my taste is for liturgical worship, but with joy and wonder—yet almost anything is preferable to the dire frigidity of much that passes for Christian praise. Certainly, the Old Testament would not recognize it as the uninhibited worship of the God of all the earth.

God is to be praised, our psalm says, because he is 'great' and 'above all gods'. Every other allegiance is challenged by our allegiance to him, and praise establishes our priority: reality above idolatry. God is to be praised as the creator who 'made the heavens', and for his divine attributes, honour, majesty, strength and beauty. To such a God the people are called to 'ascribe... the [honour and] glory due his name', the name 'Yahweh', 'I AM'. It is interesting that their praise, however noisy and spontaneous, should in its splendour and awe evoke trembling. There is nothing casual or light-hearted about a true offering of praise, even when it comes from joyful lips. To praise God is the highest calling of humanity, so it is right that our praise should represent the very best that we can offer him.

A reflection

We can see two apparently contradictory facets of praise in the Old Testament: the joyful, exuberant explosion of music, shouts and dance on the one hand, and the awe and majesty of the temple and its vestments and ornaments on the other. Perhaps the greatest challenge to Christian worship is in some way to marry those two facets, so that our praise is full both of joy and awe.

26

PRIEST

Then bring near to you your brother Aaron, and his sons with him, from among the Israelites, to serve me as priests—Aaron and Aaron's sons, Nadab and Abihu, Eleazar and Ithamar. You shall make sacred vestments for the glorious adornment of your brother Aaron… So Aaron shall bear the names of the sons of Israel in the breastpiece of judgement on his heart when he goes into the holy place, for a continual remembrance before the Lord. In the breast-piece of judgment you shall put the Urim and the Thummim, and they shall be on Aaron's heart when he goes in before the Lord; thus Aaron shall bear the judgment of the Israelites on his heart before the Lord continually… You shall make a rosette of pure gold, and engrave on it, like the engraving of a signet, 'Holy to the Lord.' You shall fasten it on the turban with a blue cord; it shall be on the front of the turban. It shall be on Aaron's forehead, and Aaron shall take on himself any guilt incurred in the holy offering that the Israelites consecrate as their sacred donations; it shall always be on his forehead, in order that they may find favour before the Lord.

EXODUS 28:1–2, 29–30, 36–38

To understand the word 'priest' as it occurs in the Hebrew scriptures we must first dismiss all thoughts of modern-day ministers, priests or rabbis. The priests of Israel were a clearly defined group of people with a very specific function, and it's safe to say that there is no one in the world at the moment who is fulfilling that function. Strictly speaking, they were all descendants of Aaron, the brother of Moses, though it would seem that other members of the tribe of Levi (the 'Levites') also fulfilled what we might think of as priestly functions. During the exile, it would seem that the Levites took on a number of priestly roles, especially relating to teaching the law. The precise relationship between the priests and the Levites is something of a puzzle to Old Testament scholars, and need not concern us for the purposes of this book.

The chief function of the priest was to offer sacrifices which would redeem the people from their sins. This work was carried on at the tabernacle, in the early days, and later at the temple. There, a huge number of priests offered endless sacrifices of lambs, goats and even bullocks, as well as birds (pigeons and doves) on the part of poorer people like the parents of Jesus (see Luke 2:24). They also presented bloodless gifts and offerings of grain or fruit, as laid down in the various ritual laws, many of them to be found in Leviticus.

Perhaps the simplest way to describe the ministry of the priest was as a man who represented God to the people and the people to God. In making sacrifices and offerings, and in praying for the people, he stood before God on their behalf. In teaching and instruction, and (for the high priest) in making judgment, using the Urim and Thummim, he represented God to the people. In other words, he was an intermediary, a kind of bridge between the people in their sin and failure and God in his holiness. The ephod worn by the priests, and the breastpiece and the 'turban' with its rosette worn by the high priest, might be seen both as emphasizing the holiness of the calling and their own vulnerability before God. They were certainly not there to glorify the priest, but to emphasize that unless he were called by God and protected by his mercy, he would himself be in peril of divine judgment.

The Urim and Thummim are among the great mysteries of biblical scholarship, because nobody seems to know for certain what they were, or what they did. What does seem clear is that they were instruments or means of acquiring God's guidance. While they are often referred to, their precise function and the method of their employment is never fully explained, and in any case their use seems to have died out after the time of Ezra and Nehemiah. It would seem that they were worn, at least at times, by the high priest on his breastpiece as part of the priestly garb, the ephod, and that one of them, probably Urim, was a negative answer to an enquiry, and Thummin a positive one. With the aid of a little textual reconstruction, the NRSV, following the RSV, gets as near as possible to a demonstration of the method in use (see 1 Samuel 14:41). Saul begged the high priest for guidance over an issue of guilt: Urim to indicate that the fault was with Saul or his son Jonathan; Thummim to indicate that the guilt was the people's. Urim was revealed, and it was discovered that Jonathan had inadvertently broken a fast.

It may be that Urim and Thummim were simply flat stones, kept in the priest's pouch, which could be thrown or tossed to get a result of 'yes' or 'no', but there is no conclusive evidence. Whatever the details of procedure, it's clear that the high priest had some role in offering divine guidance to the people, representing the will of God to them.

The sacrificial priesthood ended with the destruction of the temple in AD70. From that time, Jews have practised their religion without recourse to blood sacrifices, the Day of Atonement being marked by prayers of penitence and longing for forgiveness and restoration. For Christians, as the letter to the Hebrews makes clear, the temple priesthood has now been fulfilled in the priesthood of Jesus, the great 'high priest', whose offering made once and for all is deemed sufficient atonement for the sins of the whole world and requires no repetition (Hebrews 9:11–28). When the English word 'priest' is used today of a Christian minister, it is a contraction of the Greek word *presbyter* (elder). Such a 'priestly' ministry might be seen to relate in a public or leadership way to the fundamental notion of representing God to the people and the people to God— a task now assigned to the whole Church (see 1 Peter 2:9).

Other religions have 'priests' who are referred to in the Old Testament. Moses' father-in-law was a priest of Midian, for instance —and a deeply God-fearing one. There is also the mysterious Melchizedek, who appears in the story of Abraham and is described as a 'priest of God Most High' (Genesis 14:18). He offers gifts of bread and wine to Abraham and blesses him. Melchizedek was king of Salem (probably to be identified with Jerusalem) and later, after his conquest of Jerusalem, David was acclaimed as 'a priest for ever according to the order of Melchizedek' (Psalm 110:4). As a descendant of David, Jesus is described in exactly those terms by the author of the letter to the Hebrews (5:6–11; 6:20—7:28). In general terms, the New Testament sees Jesus as fulfilling the intermediary role of the high priest, both as one who makes intercession for us, and as the sole mediator between God and humankind (1 Timothy 2:5).

A reflection

Ever since the Fall, it would seem that human beings have experienced a gulf between where they are, as fallible and sinful creatures, and where God is, dwelling in purity and holiness. The priest provided what we might think of as a temporary bridge across this gulf, but obviously the best 'bridge' would be someone who was both human (and could understand our temptations and weaknesses) and divine (and could understand the utter purity and holiness of God).

27

PROPHECY

Now the word of the Lord came to me saying, 'Before I formed you in the womb I knew you, and before you were born I consecrated you; I appointed you a prophet to the nations.' Then I said, 'Ah, Lord God! Truly I do not know how to speak, for I am only a boy.' But the Lord said to me, 'Do not say, "I am only a boy"; for you shall go to all to whom I send you, and you shall speak whatever I command you. Do not be afraid of them, for I am with you to deliver you, says the Lord.' Then the Lord put out his hand and touched my mouth; and the Lord said to me, 'Now I have put my words in your mouth.'

JEREMIAH 1:4–9

The Hebrew scriptures are often summarized as 'the law and the prophets', and certainly when you look at the Old Testament it's obvious that the books of the law, the first five, and the books of the prophets, the last 17, make up most of the whole. Even that distinction is inadequate, however, because there are prophets and prophecy in the Pentateuch (the books of the law) and in Kings and Chronicles (just think of Elijah and Elisha), and there are obviously prophetic elements in the Psalms, too. Abraham is called a prophet (Genesis 20:7) and Moses was to become the model of all the prophets, a man with whom God spoke 'face to face' and who was entrusted to deliver the Lord's words to the people (Exodus 33:11).

Those are clearly the main functions of a prophet, as is clear from the call of Jeremiah, in the passage above—to receive God's word and then speak it out. In fact, their task is to 'forth tell' rather than to 'foretell', even though modern English usage implies that a prophet is one who foretells the future. The three Hebrew words usually translated 'prophet' seem to be more or less inter-changeable, but cover the ideas of being called by God, of seeing divine truth (a 'seer') and of speaking it out. Indeed, the greatest sin for a prophet would be to possess the message but not speak it.

The biblical prophets used various means to communicate that message. Sometimes they simply preached it; sometimes they wrapped it up in an allegorical story (see, for instance, Ezekiel 16 or 23), and sometimes they acted it out in what we would nowadays call a visual aid. In fact, these acted oracles are much more than simply aids to understanding. Often in a powerful way they are themselves the message. We can think of Isaiah walking naked and barefoot to demonstrate that the Egyptians and Ethiopians would be led into exile shamelessly exposed in their nakedness (Isaiah 20). Even more dramatically, perhaps, we have the story of the dying Elisha and King Joash, whom he instructs to shoot an arrow out of the window towards the east, as a sign of victory over Aram. The king successfully does that, with a little help from the prophet's hands, but fails to understand the significance of the next acted oracle, which involves striking the ground with arrows. He only strikes the ground three times. As a result, he is told, the Arameans would be defeated only three times, whereas if he had continued striking with the arrows their defeat would have been permanent. Clearly this incident, however we read it, is more than simply a 'visual aid'.

The prophets deal in visions, of course—some, like Ezekiel's vision of the wheeled engine, are powerful and vivid but hard to interpret (1:4–28). In this sense, they are 'seers'—they 'see' what may be hidden from mortal eye. They also do look to the future, of course, often through such visions but also in very specific warnings or words of ultimate hope. None of the biblical prophets ends his message without that note of hope. They see themselves as realists, but also ultimately optimists. How could it be otherwise for those who believe that every human event, past, present and future, lies within the providential government of the Lord God?

This brings us to the subject of 'false prophets', who feature quite largely in the biblical story. Usually, they are either blind optimists or time-servers, saying what they think will please the current ruler, or the people who make up their audience. The denunciation of them is often fierce. However, the problem is recognized and real: how does one tell a false prophet from the true one—especially if both claim to speak the 'word of the Lord' and both are sure that their message is valid?

The Old Testament seems to provide a series of tests, many of which would be equally useful to a Christian who wishes to test some of the quasi-prophetic words uttered from time to time by today's preachers. Firstly, does it come to pass—because what does not come to pass cannot be a prophecy spoken by the Lord. We can see that test being applied in Deuteronomy 18. Of course, sometimes we cannot know, simply because the event or outcome still lies in the future. From time to time, however, this is a valuable and practical test, one which many Jehovah's Witnesses applied in 1972 when the visible coming of Christ prophesied by their leaders did not materialize.

A further test is whether the prophecy is consistent with the revelation of God which we have already received. We can see this being applied in Deuteronomy 13, where the false prophets draw the people after gods other than the One who brought them out of Egypt at the Exodus. A similar test is that of the prophet's own life and lifestyle. If a prophet lives an immoral life, he is not likely to call people to holy living (see Jeremiah 23:10–22). He is condemned not so much by what he says but by the life he lives. To proclaim 'peace' without any notion of repentance or amendment of life is empty optimism (Jeremiah 6:14).

For Ezekiel, the mark of the false prophet is just such a shallowness, devoid of moral content or challenge. The true prophet speaks what he hears from God, without fear or favour. It is the 'word of the Lord' and can't be distorted by empty optimism or vague promises of peace (12:21—14:11).

At times, the Hebrew prophets seem to speak in a way which is disparaging of the religious traditions and practices of Judaism.

There is plenty of scorn of sacrifices offered from hardened hearts, or feasts observed by those who are not averse to a spot of dallying with alien gods or practising greed or injustice. Amos cried out eloquently against such empty religion: 'I hate, I despise your festivals, and I take no delight in your solemn assemblies. Even though you offer me your burnt-offerings and grain-offerings, I will not accept them; and the offerings of well-being of your fatted animals I will not look upon. Take away from me the noise of your songs; I will not listen to the melody of your harps. But let justice roll down like waters, and righteousness like an ever-flowing stream' (5:21–24).

In a way, true prophecy is self-authenticating, and we can feel it in the passion of those verses. Amos was not out to please or flatter or cajole. He had a burning message, and it had to be spoken. As Jeremiah said, the Lord had put out his hand and touched his mouth. What came from it could only be 'the word of the Lord'.

A reflection

Prophecy did not end with the last of the Hebrew prophets,
but if it is claimed and practised in the Christian Church, the same
rigorous tests need to be applied to it—most of all, that it should be
self-authenticating, consistent with the revealed truth of God,
and intended to promote holy and godly living.

28

RIGHTEOUS

Happy are those
who do not follow the advice of the wicked,
or take the path that sinners tread,
or sit in the seat of scoffers;
but their delight is in the law of the Lord,
and on his law they meditate day and night.
They are like trees
planted by streams of water,
which yield their fruit in its season,
and their leaves do not wither.
In all that they do, they prosper…
For the Lord watches over the way of the righteous,
but the way of the wicked will perish.

PSALM 1:1–3, 6

In modern English, about the only time we use the word 'righteous'
is with the prefix 'self', and then usually in a negative sense: 'Oh,
don't be so self-righteous'. We would not normally think it a
compliment to call someone 'righteous' ('good', 'kind', 'thoughtful'
are more to our taste), but in its biblical use, 'righteous' is an
absolutely key word. God is righteous (Psalm 7:9b) and calls his
people to be righteous. That's to say, he is a just God who does
what is 'right', and his will is that his human creatures should do
the same. A righteous person is all of the things we would today
associate with 'being good', including kind and thoughtful, but
chiefly he or she would have as their goal doing what God requires,
living by God's standards, being just in actions and generous in
conduct. In this way, the righteous person's life is positive in terms

of a relationship both with fellow human beings and with God.

The Hebrew word probably comes from a root meaning 'straightness'. In fact, when we say of somebody today that he or she is always 'straight' with us, we are very near the heart of righteousness. (That, it seems to me, is a good reason for avoiding the term 'straight' to denote a heterosexual person as distinct from a homosexual one—in biblical terms, they may in fact be far from 'straight'!) The 'straight' heart does not deviate from what is good and virtuous; it is not seduced by evil—following 'the path that sinners tread' (v. 1b), or taking their advice, as our psalm puts it. It is, however, more than simply a negative rejection of evil; it is a positive embracing of what is good, delighting in the law of the Lord. There's no idea here of a reluctant compulsion to toe the line, more an enthusiasm for a way of life that God will honour, which will produce 'fruit' and lead to true prosperity.

To be righteous, then, is to follow the will of God, particularly, of course, as expressed in his law and commandments. For the reader of the Hebrew scriptures, those commandments were not to be seen as a burden, but as a joy, which properly followed and lived by would bring fulfilment and freedom. The whole of the long Psalm 119 spells out that message: 'See, I have longed for your precepts; in your righteousness give me life' (v. 40). Seen in this way, righteousness is a way of life, not a code of conduct.

All of this flows from the character of God himself. He is a 'righteous God and a Saviour' (Isaiah 45:21b)—in other words, his righteousness, understood and applied to our lives, will bring us wholeness ('salvation'). In the writings of Paul, this righteousness of God can only truly be received by faith in him, and he uses many Old Testament instances to prove his point, most notably Abraham, whose righteousness before God was common ground to Jew and Christian. 'His faith was reckoned to him as righteousness' (Romans 4:22)—his acts of obedience and commitment flowed from his trust in God, rather than from any intrinsic virtue of his own. Nevertheless, for Paul, as for the psalmist and all the other writers of the Hebrew scriptures, there was no evading the call to live a righteous life, a point which Jesus made with some force in the Sermon on the Mount (see, for instance, Matthew 5:20).

Perhaps the simplest way to think of righteousness in biblical terms is to equate it with the 'virtuous' life. The righteous man or woman does not ask: 'What will I get out of this?' nor even: 'What would be the consequences of such an action?' but: 'Would this be the right thing to do?' It's not difficult to think of such a person as being like a tree planted next to a river, its leaves green and its fruit rich and heavy. This, the psalmist would say, is not only the right but the best way to live—God's way.

A reflection

'[The Lord] loves righteousness and justice; the earth is full of the steadfast love of the Lord' (Psalm 33:5). Is it in responding to that 'steadfast love' that the human heart may be weaned away from what is wicked and towards what is righteous?

29

SACRIFICE

Then Noah built an altar to the Lord, and took of every clean animal and of every clean bird, and offered burnt offerings on the altar. And when the Lord smelled the pleasing odour, the Lord said in his heart, 'I will never again curse the ground because of humankind, for the inclination of the human heart is evil from youth; nor will I ever again destroy every living creature as I have done. As long as the earth endures, seedtime and harvest, cold and heat, summer and winter, day and night, shall not cease.'
GENESIS 8:20–22

We have already considered the role of offerings and sacrifices in the worship of Israel (under 'Offering'), so this chapter will concentrate on the basic idea of sacrifice. Our reading tells us that from the earliest times, the human race felt some deep inner need to make sacrifices to the deity. Indeed, in the biblical story of creation there is at least a hint that the clothing God made for Adam and Eve from animal skins, after their sinful rebellion against his will, anticipated the use of sacrifices for the purpose of atonement for sin (Genesis 3:21). Be that as it may, in the story of their two sons Abel and Cain there can be little doubt that Abel's offering to God was of an animal sacrifice, while Cain's less acceptable one was of grain or fruit (Genesis 4:1–5). The passage at the head of this chapter relates the sacrifices offered by Noah in thanksgiving after the flood receded. Apparently the 'smell' of these burnt offerings was pleasing to the Lord, who in response uttered his first covenant promise—that despite human sin he would never again curse the ground because of it, but let the seasons roll by in their appointed order, including seed-time and harvest, 'as long as the earth endures'.

Whatever meaning we wish to give to these ancient stories, they certainly make it clear that the principle of sacrifice—blood-offerings—was rooted in human religious consciousness from the earliest times. Probably the priestly editors of these early books wished to establish the antiquity of that principle, which was to become the bedrock of Israel's worship. We can imagine that at the time there was little need to justify the practice: its logic seemed self-evident. Sin was serious, indeed mortally wounding. 'The person who sins shall die' (Ezekiel 18:20a). Therefore a death was required to atone for sin, and if it was not to be the death of the sinner then it would have to be the death of a substitute—normally, a lamb or goat, though of course in the practice of some of the tribes of those days human sacrifices were not uncommon. As the author of the letter to the Hebrews puts it, writing in the New Testament but about the temple sacrifices, 'Without the shedding of blood there is no forgiveness of sins' (9:22b).

That was the principle of sacrifices for sin. But there were also sacrifices offered purely for worship and thanksgiving. Abel's and Noah's sacrifices would have fallen into this category. Here the notion, surely, is of value. If I am truly and genuinely grateful for something I have received, I demonstrate my appreciation by offering to the donor something of similar value as a costly gift. As King David put it, in rejecting the offer of animals without cost for sacrifice, 'I will not offer burnt-offerings to the Lord my God that cost me nothing' (2 Samuel 24:24b).

In the ancient world, these sacrifices would almost certainly be animals from the flocks. It may seem to the modern reader a crude, even barbarous notion. Our sensitivity shrinks from the thought of an endless procession of innocent animals being led to slaughter for no other reason than either to placate or express gratitude to the deity. On the other hand, we may well recognize that the feeling of guilt, on the one hand, or of dependence, on the other, could only be expressed by as costly a gesture as this.

In any case, in the ordinary course of modern life, we are aware that a costly gift means more than a cheap one. To mark our love, devotion or gratitude we may well spend rather more on a gift than we can sensibly afford. It was costly, very costly, to a subsistence farmer to give animals from his herds (or, for that matter, bunches of grapes from his vines) as offerings to God, but it was certainly a way to show the reality of gratitude or, of course, in the case of sacrifices, repentance for sin.

The time would come in the history of Israel when the sacrificial system became simply that—a system. The later Hebrew prophets can get very indignant about meaningless sacrifices offered from unrepentant hearts. Isaiah was scathing on the subject: '"The multitude of your sacrifices—what are they to me?" says the Lord. "I have more than enough of burnt offerings... Stop doing wrong, learn to do right!"' (Isaiah 1:11, 16–17, NIV).

A reflection

In any language, a sacrifice is something that costs us something. We may sacrifice money, or time, or skill, or energy to a cause or to prove our devotion to a person. The practice of sacrificing animals to God may seem alien to our way of thinking, but at least we should be able to see that it was not an empty gesture if the heart of the donor was right and the cost of the gift was great. Christians will want to think of the sacrifice of Jesus, the 'Lamb of God' (John 1:36b)—a sacrifice which was both his and the Father's, and of infinite cost.

30

SALVATION

'I will give you as a light to the nations,
that my salvation may reach to the end of the earth.'
Thus says the Lord,
the Redeemer of Israel and his Holy One,
to one deeply despised, abhorred by the nations,
the slave of rulers,
'Kings shall see and stand up,
princes, and they shall prostrate themselves,
because of the Lord, who is faithful,
the Holy One of Israel, who has chosen you.'
Thus says the Lord:
'In a time of favour I have answered you,
on a day of salvation I have helped you;
I have kept you and given you
as a covenant to the people,
to establish the land,
to apportion the desolate heritages;
saying to the prisoners, "Come out",
to those who are in darkness, "Show yourselves."
They shall feed along the ways,
on all the bare heights shall be their pasture;
they shall not hunger or thirst,
neither scorching wind nor sun shall strike them down,
for he who has pity on them will lead them,
and by springs of water will guide them.

ISAIAH 49:6B–10

When Christians use the word 'salvation' they do so in a religious or spiritual sense—salvation is the gift of God, forgiveness, wholeness, eternal life. In the Old Testament, however, it has a much wider and less specifically 'religious' connotation: salvation is to be saved, in the sense of rescued or delivered—from sickness and death, from our enemies, from famine. That does not by any means exhaust its meaning for the writers, but it sets the ground rules. God is their unique Saviour, and every blessing and every deliverance from evil comes from him. By natural extension, that includes spiritual blessings, including forgiveness and, especially in the great Hebrew prophets, the hope that in the future he would bring his people into a new and rewarding experience of his love and blessing. The fact remains that the Hebrew and Christian scriptures have a different emphasis where this word is concerned, which should be borne in mind when we are reading the Psalms, for instance.

The principal Hebrew word translated 'salvation' carries the idea of being delivered or rescued. It is often used of deliverance from disease (Isaiah 38:20), from enemies (Psalm 44:7) or from trouble (Jeremiah 3:23). Its model, for Israel, was the rescue from slavery in Egypt. That was seen as the ultimate act of salvation, the deliverance of God's people from captivity and their ultimate arrival in the land of promise, 'flowing with milk and honey'. Always and uniquely God is the Saviour. As second Isaiah puts it in the words of God, 'I am the Lord, and besides me there is no Saviour' (43:11). In the Exodus story, that element is paramount. It was by God's strength, his 'stretched out arm', that the people were delivered from Egypt— indeed, they were not called to strike a single blow in their own cause, so that they could have no reason to claim that 'they' had conquered the might of Egypt. What they sang and celebrated across the Red Sea was the salvation of God, his unmerited blessing brought about by his limitless power. There, in microcosm, is the Old Testament doctrine of salvation.

The Hebrew scriptures, and especially the later prophets, do introduce another element, however, a salvation which for them still lay in the future. This would come about in the fullness of time, at

God's appointed hour, and it would involve a rather deeper concept of salvation, rather nearer the idea of spiritual 'wholeness' which lies behind the New Testament use of the word. In the later chapters of Isaiah, for instance, we begin to see the hope of a new world at the end of the present age, in Hebrew 'olam habba'. It is this new world that the prophet is foretelling in the passage from Isaiah 49. In this new era, God would reign in righteousness and justice in a golden age of blessing. It was in this setting that the Hebrew scriptures developed the concept of messiahship, because it would be through the anointed One of God, the Messiah, that true salvation would eventually come: on God's behalf, he would be their Saviour.

This salvation would not simply be for the historic people of Israel, either. This was for the whole world, the 'nations' (v. 6b). All would see God's glory, and all would know his blessing. At last, Israel would see the true fulfilment of the promise made to Abraham, that through this people all the nations of the earth would be blessed (Genesis 22:18). In the Isaiah passage above, kings and princes (v. 7) will on that day acknowledge the Lord and see that Israel's covenant is for the blessing of all people. In that way, salvation would fulfil its root meaning of freedom from limitation. All people would be set free, but free to know and serve the God of their salvation.

A reflection

'To you is born this day in the city of David a Saviour, who is the Messiah, the Lord' (Luke 2:11). It is quite hard to understand the full impact of the words of the angel to the shepherds announcing the birth of Jesus without at least some understanding of what those shepherds would have understood by the word 'saviour'. God is the only Saviour, so it was God who, in a mysterious way, must have come to be their deliverer. No wonder they went 'with haste' to see 'this thing that has taken place' (Luke 2:15–16)!

31

SERVANT

Here is my servant, whom I uphold,
my chosen, in whom my soul delights;
I have put my spirit upon him;
he will bring forth justice to the nations.
He will not cry or lift up his voice,
or make it heard in the street;
a bruised reed he will not break,
and a dimly burning wick he will not quench;
he will faithfully bring forth justice.
He will not grow faint or be crushed
until he has established justice in the earth;
and the coastlands wait for his teaching.

ISAIAH 42:1–4

Most of us have never had a servant, and our knowledge of their ways is restricted to television and films. Still, even from that we can create an impression of the faithful retainer, hovering at his master's elbow ready to pick up his stick or brush the dandruff off his collar, or the maid nervously adjusting her mistress's veil. Servants serve, and from that we get the word 'servile', meaning 'slavish' or 'fawning'. The modern employee, with protected rights in law, is really nothing like the old idea of the servant, just as the modern employer is not, or should not be, remotely like the feudal lord who treated his servants like robots programmed to do his bidding.

All of that makes it quite hard for us to understand fully the role of the servant in the life of ancient Israel. Abraham's family, for instance, is deemed to include not only his wife or wives and children, but also his 'menservants and maidservants' (Genesis

24:35, KJV). Although they possessed no legal rights, and in some cases were little more than slaves, they were part of the household, dependent on the master, but often having a genuine loyalty and affection for him and their mistress.

Such servants were often given tasks of enormous responsibility. Abraham in his old age charged his servant, 'the oldest of his house, who had charge of all that he had', to find a wife for his son Isaac from among his kindred, rather than from the local Canaanite women (Genesis 24:1–4). In order to do that, the servant was sent off laden with treasure and costly gifts, and given the sole responsibility of finding the 'right' woman. This task he duly achieved with wonderful tact, skill and diplomacy, finding the beautiful Rebekah at a well, negotiating with her father and making all the arrangements for the betrothal and dowry. The story is told in sumptuous detail, yet this magnificent servant is never even dignified with a name!

The whole incident helps to show the role of the loyal and dedicated servant of the master, which was to become a picture of the relationship of Israel to the Lord God. They were to be his servants; he was to be their Lord. They would serve him, but he would honour and bless them. They were a servant nation. It was an arrangement which the people could understand and think of in terms of a master–servant relationship.

Many great figures in the Old Testament are called 'servants of the Lord God, Yahweh'. They include Abraham (Genesis 26:24), Jacob (Ezekiel 28:25b), Joshua (Joshua 24:29a) and David (Psalm 144:10b). Here, it is obviously a complimentary term, denoting a person who is loyal and faithful to God. In general usage in the Hebrew scriptures, the title is used of civil servants, military officers, ambassadors and courtiers—certainly not people normally regarded as inferior, let alone slaves. So the term could be used as high praise for someone's loyalty, while at the same time sometimes being applied to people of high rank as a humiliation. When Hazael came to the prophet Elisha from King Ben-hadad of Aram as his envoy, he was told that he, as a future king, would do evil to the people of Israel. 'What is your servant', Hazael responded, 'who is a mere dog, that he should do this great thing?' (2 Kings 8:13a). In one short sentence, he was both a servant of the prophet and a 'mere dog'!

So there were servants in households and royal courts, and there was the servant-nation, Israel. Yet our reading from second Isaiah seems to speak of the servant of the Lord as an individual. This person will be chosen by God (like Israel), but will act gently and generously, not with raised voice or flamboyant actions, in order to establish justice in the earth—indeed, for all the nations.

This identification of the servant of the Lord with a charismatic individual is a characteristic of the so-called 'servant songs' of this section of Isaiah (see 42:1–4; 49:1–6; 50:4–9; 52:13—56:12). The identity of this servant of the Lord has been disputed over the years. Is he a kind of personification of obedient Israel? Is he the prophet, seeing himself as a loyal messenger to a burdened people? Or is he, as Christians have normally read it, the Messiah of God? If it is the last, then we have here a radically different notion of messiahship: not a restored monarch in the Davidic line, not a mighty ruler, not an anointed Aaronic priest, but a despised and rejected servant who would suffer and die for the people, who would be 'wounded for our transgressions, crushed for our iniquities' and on whom 'the Lord has laid... the iniquity of us all' (53:5, 6). In the light of this, it is hardly surprising that Christians have seen Jesus as the fulfilment of this prophecy. Indeed, he seems to have always seen his own messiahship in terms of the suffering servant rather than the conquering king.

There is not necessarily a great conflict between the idea of Israel as the servant of the Lord and an individual figure being chosen by God as representing and embodying all that Israel was meant to be. The promise to Abraham was that through his descendants the whole earth would be blessed. The nation thought of itself as inheriting that promise, but the insistent message of the later prophets of Israel was that they had forfeited the role through disobedience—though they also held out the prospect of a future when the blessings of the covenant would be restored. The servant songs of Isaiah propose a new way, the coming of an individual who sums up in himself all that Israel was intended to represent and yet has a mission to Israel (see Isaiah 49:5–13). This person would perfectly fulfil the purpose of God.

It is not by any means only Christians who have identified this figure with the Messiah. It is also the traditional Jewish interpretation, and certainly in later Palestinian Judaism, which prevailed during the New Testament period. Some Jewish scholars, however, did find deeply embarrassing the idea of a messiah who suffered in the kind of way Isaiah 53 describes. In fact, the Targum of Jonathan—a fourth-century AD Aramaic version of parts of the Old Testament—drastically reconstructs the text to remove this element from it, partly no doubt because of the interpretation which the rapidly growing Christian Church was putting on it.

None of that detracts from the fundamental dignity of the role of the Lord's servant, nor of the responsibility it places on those who are called to it. Israel found it both a blessing and a burden, but will surely one day find that this Master, unlike some earthly ones, is generous, patient and utterly faithful to those he has called to serve him.

A reflection

Is Mary's the perfect prayer: 'Here am I, the servant of the Lord; let it be with me according to your word' (Luke 1:38a)?

32

SIN

> Have mercy on me, O God,
> according to your steadfast love;
> according to your abundant mercy
> blot out my transgressions.
> Wash me thoroughly from my iniquity,
> and cleanse me from my sin.
> For I know my transgressions,
> and my sin is ever before me.
> Against you, you alone, have I sinned,
> and done what is evil in your sight,
> so that you are justified in your sentence
> and blameless when you pass judgement.
>
> PSALM 51:1–4

The word 'sin' hardly figures in today's vocabulary. Until a few years ago, it eked out an existence in the strange phrase 'living in sin' to describe unmarried couples living together. Now, even that usage has gone, and we are simply left with an empty idea, a word virtually without meaning for most people. The Church continues to use it, of course, which leads occasional visitors to allege that Christians are 'out of touch with modern thinking'. Possibly as a result, preachers tend to steer clear of its use, emphasizing instead the positive benefits of faith, rather than the promise of forgiveness of sin.

You can't get far in the Bible without encountering sin—not merely the word, but also the concept. Adam and Eve sinned in the garden by disobedience; their son Cain by giving way to envy, and it is said of the people of Noah's generation that 'every inclination of the thoughts of their hearts was only evil continually' (Genesis 6:5b). The Hebrew scriptures offer no explanation for its origin in a world which God had created to be 'very good'. The implication is that the possibility of disobedience must always be present when obedience is being called for, and that human beings, perhaps out of curiosity, could not resist the temptation (note the word) to explore evil as well as good (see, for instance, Genesis 3:5). The Bible simply takes the existence, or at least the possibility, of evil for granted, and proceeds to tell the story of the slow unfolding of God's purpose to overcome it.

Not surprisingly, in view of the many ways in which it manifests itself, Hebrew has a choice of words which at different times can be translated as 'sin'. The most common conveys the idea of deviating from the target, 'missing the mark'. Usually the 'mark' in question is a divine precept or command, and to miss it is in fact to fall short of God's requirements.

Another word emphasizes the nature of sin as deliberate wrongdoing. This word is often translated in older versions of the Bible as 'iniquity': the perversion or distortion of what is known to be right. Another word sees sin as deviation from the true path, 'going astray', and yet another to acting wickedly.

Perhaps the most solemn of all the Hebrew words for sin is the tiny word *ps*, which speaks of sin as rebellion against God and the open defiance of his kingly rule. Sinners are, in other words, rebels and traitors: 'Rebels and sinners shall be destroyed together' (Isaiah 1:28a).

So much for the terminology. The variety of use can be seen in the passage from Psalm 51: 'transgressions', 'iniquity', 'sin', 'evil'. All may be used to describe the writer's sense of shame and accountability to God. Traditionally, this psalm is ascribed to David 'when the prophet Nathan came to him, after he had gone in to Bathsheba'—in other words, at a moment of deep conviction of wrongdoing: adultery, and then what amounted to manslaughter. In it, he sees each facet of his sin: it is disobedience of God's commands; it is rebellion against God's will; it falls far short of his moral requirements; it has led David away from the true path; a distortion of what is right. Individually or added together, they paint the same sombre picture: sin is serious.

That is probably the heart of the Old Testament's teaching about sin. It is always sin against God ('against you, you alone, have I sinned', v. 4) and hence it is serious. The people would be deluded if they thought that their holy God could simply overlook it. It was a corruption of his creation and a perversion of his people. The most common term used to describe his reaction to these manifestations of sin is 'anger' or 'wrath'. In an intensified form, it becomes 'fierce wrath' (see, for example, Exodus 32:9–12).

We must be clear that this is not simply petulance or annoyance. The wrath of God is a profound displeasure at the corruption of his purpose or the rejection of his love. It is certainly not vindictive, but directed towards human repentance and restoration. Yet we could say that it is implacable, on the principle that sin tolerated would eventually destroy his most loved and treasured possession and corrupt the universe that he had brought into being. In fact, the purpose of God is the total eradication from his creation of everything that corrupts and defiles it (see Revelation 21:27).

If the first principle of the Old Testament about sin is its seriousness, perhaps the second is the fact that it inevitably has consequences. There is no such thing as a harmless sin (however much we may wish there were), because to operate against God's will and purpose, which is the essence of sin, is either to harm ourselves or to harm others. Children usually begin to learn at quite an early age that actions have consequences, but sometimes we seem to grow out of this realization. 'Be sure your sin will find you out' (Numbers 32:23b) might well be written at the front of all our diaries!

A third principle should also be mentioned. God is a God of mercy and forgiveness, in the Old Testament as in the New. Time and again the people of Israel test his patient love but never reach its limits. As they turn to him and repent of their sin, so he forgives and restores them. It is, in a nutshell, the story of the whole Bible.

If it were not so, then sin would have conquered love; evil would have defeated goodness—and that is unthinkable.

A reflection

When David said that his sin was ever before him, he was describing the work of a divinely activated conscience. Perhaps it is only when, like him, we know our transgressions and feel unable to close our eyes to their existence that we shall seriously deal with them.

33

SLAVERY

I am the Lord your God, who brought you out of the land of Egypt, out of the house of slavery; you shall have no other gods before [or, besides] me.

EXODUS 20:2–3

The Old Testament records two forms of slavery. The first is personal slavery, which was common among the Israelites and indeed throughout the society of the time. Some people were born slaves, being the children of parents who were slaves. Some fell into slavery through debt, usually over land. And some became slaves simply through poverty or circumstance. As we have already seen (under 'Servant'), the slave was regarded as a member of the master's household and enjoyed his protection, but had no legal rights with regard to conditions of work, hours of employment, or pay. However, as stipulated in the law, slaves were free from work on the sabbath, which was at least an advance on the situation in most of the surrounding nations.

According to the law of Moses, Hebrew slaves (but not foreign ones) were entitled to be released in the jubilee year, which fell when seven times seven years had passed (in other words, seven sabbaths) of years. At that point, the slave should also receive the restoration of his inheritance (see Leviticus 25:28, 40). Those who fell into slavery through debt were to be released from bondage in the seventh year, again with the provision of sufficient resources to enable them to make a new start (Leviticus 25; Exodus 21:2–6). These generous provisions, by the standards of the ancient world, were probably not universally applied. Jeremiah denounces the practice of releasing the slaves, in line with the seventh year law, but then immediately taking them back into servitude—a flagrant breach of the divine commands (see 34:13–16). Some scholars believe that the whole principle of jubilee was either never fully practised, or was quickly abandoned as economically unacceptable.

In any case, foreign slaves had no such rights and could be enslaved permanently—and even passed on as part of the owner's property to his descendants. There were a number of laws and instructions regarding the treatment of slaves in Israel, most of which to the modern reader seem thoughtless and harsh. For instance, if an owner strikes a slave, male or female, with a stick, injuring them so severely that they die, there is an (unspecified) penalty. If the slave survives the attack for two days, however, there is no penalty of any kind, 'for the slave is the owner's property' (Exodus 21:21). It must be said, in the interests of truth, that even these rules were a good deal kinder than those which applied in most of the neighbouring countries.

This general background of slavery colours a great deal of biblical language, of course. To fall into slavery, whether by choice (because the alternative was starvation), purchase or inheritance, was a fate every free-born person wished to avoid. To kidnap a person and reduce them to slavery was a very serious offence in Israel (Exodus 21:16) and in other societies, too. The behaviour of Joseph's brothers in selling him off as a slave into Egypt was therefore criminal as well as morally indefensible, which may help to explain their fear when they were finally exposed before him (Genesis 45:3).

The longer-term outcome of their actions was to shape the history of the people of Israel, of course. Long after Joseph's death, his descendants ceased to be welcome and honoured guests in Egypt and were reduced to virtual slavery, being employed by Pharaoh to build his treasure-palaces. It was this 'house of slavery' from which God, through the agency of Moses, delivered them, and it was that liberation which for ever marked out the Israelites as a 'redeemed' people. Still today, in the Passover, Jews remember with thanksgiving that their ancestors were freed from slavery in Egypt through the intervention of God. 'I am the Lord your God, who brought you out of the… house of slavery'. The next clause of that statement could well be preceded by the word 'therefore'— '*therefore* you shall have no other gods beside me'. Like slaves freed by a generous benefactor, they are under a permanent debt of gratitude. Indeed, they were freed from cruel bondage to a tyrant, in order to enter into willing bondage to a loving and generous creator God.

A reflection

So with us [Christians]; while we were minors, we were enslaved to the elemental spirits of the world. But when the fullness of time had come, God sent his Son, born of a woman, born under the law, in order to redeem those who were under the law, so that we might receive adoption as children. And because you are children, God has sent the Spirit of his Son into our hearts, crying, 'Abba! Father!' So you are no longer a slave but a child, and if a child then also an heir, through God (Galatians 4:3–7).

34

TABERNACLE

The Lord said to Moses: 'Tell the Israelites to take for me an offering; from all whose hearts prompt them to give you shall receive the offering for me... And have them make me a sanctuary, so that I may dwell among them. In accordance with all that I show you concerning the pattern of the tabernacle and of all its furniture, so you shall make it.'

EXODUS 25:1–2, 8–9

As the Israelites made their way across the wilderness on their journey to the Promised Land, their worship of God seems to have taken place in a large portable tent, called the 'tent of meeting'. This arrangement became formal and regulated after Sinai, when it became known as the 'tabernacle' and strict rules were laid down about the way in which it was to be transported and erected at the various stopping-places. The honour of dismantling, carrying and erecting what sounds like a large and unwieldy piece of apparatus fell to the Levites, though whether they always saw it as an honour when they were sweating under the desert sun to manhandle its bars, posts, linens, curtains and furniture—not to mention the ark of the covenant, which was to be part of it—may seem unlikely.

After the Israelites settled in Canaan, the tabernacle had several semi-permanent resting-places (at Shiloh, Nob and Gibeon) before being brought into the temple in the time of Solomon (1 Kings 8:4). Its various names in Hebrew are probably the best indications of its meaning and purpose. It was *miskan*, which simply means 'dwelling' (that is the word used in the passage above). This signified the tent or tabernacle as the place of God's presence with his people—though, as Solomon himself made clear, their view of

God was not so unsophisticated that they thought the Lord of heaven and earth actually lived there. Nevertheless, it was also *bet Yahweh*, the 'house of the Lord God', or *miskan Yahweh*, the dwelling of the Lord God. Its importance as the place where the ark of the covenant rested and remained is expressed in other titles: *miskan ha edut*, the 'dwelling of the testimony' or the 'terms of the covenant', or *miqdas*, 'sanctuary' and *qodwa*, 'holy place'. All of these names were added over many years to enhance the simple, original title *ohel mo'ed*, 'tent of meeting'.

What do we get from this, beyond an array of mysterious Hebrew words? The answer surely is an impression of a location which was at once sacred and also a kind of rendezvous. Nothing could be more holy and awesome than the presence of the living God, Yahweh, but this presence was in the midst of his people. As they went about their work, or passed by on their travels, they could see in this structure a visible sign of that presence. Here, in the heart of the tabernacle, stood the ark of the covenant. This was a rectangular box, with a lid of solid gold bearing at each end a carved golden cherub with outstretched wings. Inside the box, as originally stipulated, were the two tablets bearing the Ten Commandments, the pot of manna and Aaron's rod. The ark rested in the 'most holy place', the innermost sanctuary of the tabernacle. Opposite it stood the altar of sacrifice and alongside it, on the north side, the table of the 'bread of the presence', or the 'shewbread'. On the south side stood the *m'norah*, the seven-branched candlestand. So the furnishings and the rituals associated with the tabernacle signified the roots of the religion of Israel: the covenant confirmed in the law, the forgiveness of sin through penitence and sacrifice and a God who is both gloriously 'other' and yet wonderfully 'present'. It was to be a constant reminder that he was their God and they were his people.

The ark and the altar were, as has been said, located in the 'most holy place', sometimes called the 'holy of holies', which was the inner of two compartments to the tabernacle. In so far as we can take these kinds of statistics literally, it would seem that the whole tabernacle was about 20 metres long. Of this, the first compartment, the 'holy place', was ten metres long and the 'most holy place' five. The width seems to have been five metres. The two compartments were divided by a heavy curtain, the 'veil', through which the high priest passed on the Day of Atonement—the veil of the temple, which was torn in two 'from top to bottom' as Jesus died (Matthew 27:51). The tabernacle itself seems to have stood in a much larger compound, perhaps 50 by 25 metres, itself bounded by a linen screen, with a gate at the east end.

The ark of the covenant, which was by far the most significant element of the whole edifice, symbolizing, as it did, the presence of God among his people, was placed in the temple with great ceremony in the reign of Solomon (1 Kings 8:1) but was presumably lost during the Babylonian desecration of the temple in the sixth century BC. There was certainly no ark in the second temple, the one which Jesus would have known.

It's not hard to see how the symbolism of the tabernacle helped to shape the religion and worship of Israel. God was with them in the wilderness, in the simple 'tent of meeting', and he was still with his people at the place of offerings and sacrifices. They knew that the whole universe was his dwelling-place, but they also knew that he had promised that his presence would go with them (Exodus 33:14), and this curtained chapel was simply a visible sign of it.

A reflection

It is rather strange to think that Christian churches have frequently been called 'tabernacles' or the 'house of God'. Many of the ones who use these titles would not really approve of the ornate fittings and furniture of the original tabernacle. They certainly wouldn't welcome them on their premises today! It is a profound truth, though, that every place where God's people meet is a 'tabernacle', a 'tent of meeting', and miskan Yahweh, *the house of God.*

35

TEST (TEMPTATION)

Vindicate me, O Lord,
for I have walked in my integrity,
and I have trusted in the Lord without wavering.
Prove me, O Lord, and try me;
test my heart and mind.
For your steadfast love is before my eyes,
and I walk in faithfulness to you.

PSALM 26:1–3

O that today you would listen to his voice!
Do not harden your hearts, as at Meribah,
as on the day at Massah in the wilderness,
when your ancestors tested me,
and put me to the proof, though they had seen my work.
For forty years I loathed that generation
and said, 'They are a people whose hearts go astray,
and they do not regard my ways.'
Therefore in my anger I swore,
'They shall not enter my rest.'

PSALM 95:7b–11

Do not put the Lord your God to the test,
as you tested him at Massah.

DEUTERONOMY 6:16

All through the Bible, 'test' and 'temptation' describe the same thing, even though in modern English we may think of them as completely different in meaning. We 'test' a potential car driver, or a vacuum cleaner we are thinking of buying. We are 'tempted' by a bar of chocolate or cash someone has left lying around. When there was an attempt to introduce a new version of the Lord's Prayer with the petition, 'Do not put us to the test' (or 'time of trial'), people were quite outraged, even though it was a far more accurate translation of the words of Jesus. To be tempted, in biblical language, is to be tested, whether by God or by some other influence. We are 'put to the test', which is what the psalmist in our passage is inviting God to do to him in order to demonstrate his integrity. Sometimes, however, the 'test' comes from another source, possibly God's 'adversary', Satan—as in Genesis 3, where the 'serpent' is commonly assumed to be satanic—and in the 'temptation' or testing of Jesus (Matthew 4:1).

In the wilderness journey, the Israelites were frequently put to the test. That's to say, their faith and trust in God were examined, usually by external circumstances—and most often they failed the test. The second of the passages above is a reminder of the incident at Rephidim, when the people quarrelled with Moses, demanding that he should give them water—indeed, they asked 'Is the Lord among us or not?' (Exodus 17:7). In the event, they were provided with water when Moses, on God's instructions, struck a rock-face with his staff, but their behaviour was seen as a failure of trust—they 'put the Lord to the test'. For that reason, the site was renamed Massah and Meribah, which mean 'test' and 'quarrel'. In Jewish tradition, that incident was held up as an example of failure of faith. Rather like a small child who deliberately sets out to irritate his mother (throwing the dummy out of the pram is the classic example) to see if she really loves him, people are prone to put God to the test. Is he really there? Does he truly care for us? Will he let me down? Even if not in those words, some of our prayers seem to get dangerously close to that.

It is true that there were occasions in the history of God's people when the Lord was 'put to the test' and it was not deemed to be sinful. Gideon's fleece is an example. Called by the Lord to deliver the people from the threat of the Midianites, Gideon feels unable to go ahead with this monumental task without further divine assurances. Here is the account from the book of Judges: 'Then Gideon said to God, "In order to see whether you will deliver Israel by my hand, as you have said, I am going to lay a fleece of wool on the threshing-floor; if there is dew on the fleece alone, and it is dry on all the ground, then I shall know that you will deliver Israel by my hand, as you have said." And it was so. When he rose early next morning and squeezed the fleece, he wrung enough dew from the fleece to fill a bowl with water. Then Gideon said to God, "Do not let your anger burn against me, let me speak one more time; let me, please, make trial with the fleece just once more; let it be dry only on the fleece, and on all the ground let there be dew." And God did so that night. It was dry on the fleece only, and on all the ground there was dew' (6:36–40).

We might feel that this was an extreme example of putting God to the test—not once, but twice! Yet clearly Gideon's actions did not meet with divine disapproval. In fact, emboldened by this assurance, he was able to lead a small company of hand-picked soldiers to rout the powerful army of Midian. The difference between this incident and the one at Rephidim seems to have been one of responsibility. The Israelites in the wilderness had already had abundant proof of God's provision. They had been taken across the Red Sea and fed with manna. God had accepted responsibility, through his servant Moses, for their safety and welfare. All they needed to do was trust him. Gideon, on the other hand, was being called by God to a new and daunting assignment. Rather like Moses at the burning bush, he sought assurance that this was truly a divine commission, and in this incident of the fleece he was given it. God had met the 'test', and now expected Gideon to do the same.

Putting God to the test is one side of the coin, so to speak. What about God putting us to the test? This is something the psalmist actually welcomed: 'Prove me, O Lord, and try me; test my heart and mind' (Psalm 26:2). Not many of us would be that confident of our 'integrity', perhaps! Yet in a way, the process goes on in the life of the disciple, whether we invite it or not. What we commonly call 'temptation' could equally well, and rather more accurately, be thought of as divine testing. God does not tempt us. That can be said categorically. 'No one, when tempted, should say, "I am being tempted by God"; for God cannot be tempted by evil and he himself tempts no one' (James 1:13). Temptation to evil comes from within the human heart. We are 'tempted by... [our] own desire, being lured and enticed by it' (James 1:14). Both of those statements are entirely consistent with the teaching of the Old as well as the New Testament. God does not tempt us to evil, but God does allow us to be put to the test. He did it to Abraham, in the strange incident of the sacrifice of Isaac (Genesis 22), just as he did it to the Hebrew people in the wilderness. In one sense he did it to Jesus, who was 'led up by the Spirit into the wilderness to be tempted by the devil' (Matthew 4:1). God was not the 'tempter', but he did lead his Son into the place of testing. There is no sin involved in being put to the test. The sin is in failing it.

We do not, or should not, put God to the test because that is to doubt his most fundamental quality, faithfulness. We do not, or should not, resist the idea of God putting us to the test, because only in that way can we learn to resist what is wrong and embrace what is right.

A reflection

'In this you rejoice, even if now for a little while you have had to suffer various trials, so that the genuineness of your faith—being more precious than gold that, though perishable, is tested by fire— may be found to result in praise and glory and honour when Jesus Christ is revealed' (1 Peter 1:6–7). Only through the testing is the pure gold of faith revealed.

36

THANKS (THANKSGIVING)

Make a joyful noise to the Lord, all the earth.
Worship the Lord with gladness;
come into his presence with singing.
Know that the Lord is God.
It is he that made us, and we are his;
we are his people, and the sheep of his pasture.
Enter his gates with thanksgiving,
and his courts with praise.
Give thanks to him, bless his name.
For the Lord is good;
his steadfast love endures for ever,
and his faithfulness to all generations.

PSALM 100

This psalm is entitled 'A Psalm of Thanksgiving', but we hardly need to be told. From first to last, it simply echoes one theme: God is good; we are his; he is ours—so let's celebrate!

This is a familiar theme in the Psalter, and indeed whenever the praises of Israel are being described. Sometimes the word 'thanksgiving' is shorthand for a sacrifice of gratitude, an offering at the altar made as an expression of thanks for a particular act of mercy or answered prayer. Equally often it applies to a general expression of gratitude to God, or to the praises of the people in the temple. It is impressive that at a time when life was undoubtedly hard for many people, with much poverty and the prospect of a poor harvest and consequent shortages ever-present, their approach to God seems to have been much more centred on thanksgiving than ours is, in our far more secure and affluent society.

This psalm sets out like a catechism the reasons for such gratitude. The most fundamental reason is that the Lord (that is, Yahweh) is God. The God of Abraham, Isaac and Jacob, the God of their fathers, is the true and only divinity. This could be taken as nationalistic pride ('Our god is better than your god!'), but in fact seems to be based not on tribal prejudice or loyalty, but on the principle of revelation. The Lord Yahweh had revealed himself to their forefathers. He had made a covenant with Abraham, the father of the nation. He had appeared to Moses at the burning bush, confirming there his unique name: Yahweh, I am—the God of time and of eternity.

He should also be thanked for his acts of creation. 'It is he that made us'. That in itself is a remarkable statement of faith, recognizing that if God is the creator then everything that exists is part of the creation—and we are creatures, with all that that involves. Some ancient manuscripts add after: 'It is he that made us' its negative corollary: 'and not we ourselves', thus emphasizing our utter dependence on him as the source of our existence. This is a healthy corrective to some modern thinking, which sees human beings as the apex of creation and our will as sovereign.

Then, as a matter of thanksgiving, because he made us 'we are his people, and the sheep of his pasture' (v. 3b). This introduces the beautiful picture of God as our 'shepherd'. The idea may echo the choice of David as king, chosen while he was still a shepherd boy caring for the flock out on the hills around Bethlehem. In any case, it emphasizes God as one who cares for his people, guides and protects them. 'The Lord is my shepherd, I shall not want. He makes me lie down in green pastures; he leads me beside still waters… He leads me in right paths for his name's sake' (Psalm 23:1–3). This speaks not only of God's care for his people, but their dependence on him, like the dependence of the helpless, scatty sheep on their shepherd. 'All we like sheep have gone astray' (Isaiah 53:6)—and anyone who has lived in Wales, for instance, will know how stupid and apparently wilful a sheep separated from the flock can be! For God to be called 'shepherd' (and for Jesus to give himself the same title) is to turn the usual notions of monarchy at the time upside down. Our God is a shepherd to his flock; we are the 'sheep of his pasture'.

Finally, the psalmist summarizes the reasons for thanksgiving by listing the fundamental qualities of Yahweh as the people of Israel had experienced them over the centuries. He is 'good'—not as obvious a statement as it may seem, given the nature of some of the 'gods' of the surrounding nations, a few of whom even required human sacrifice in order to be placated. His 'steadfast love'—*hesed*, 'loving-kindness'—'endures for ever', his people can rely on it, even when they have failed him. And, above all, as we have seen, he is 'faithful'. The God of their fathers would 'keep faith' not just for the present, but 'to all generations'. There is no time limit on the faithfulness of God.

Each of these, and all of them taken together, are ample justification for entering the gates of the temple courts with thanksgiving. This God, *our* God, deserves endless gratitude.

A reflection

For Christians, as well as for the Jewish people of old, an attitude of gratitude transforms one's whole view of life.

WILDERNESS

The wilderness and the dry land shall be glad,
the desert shall rejoice and blossom;
like the crocus it shall blossom abundantly,
and rejoice with joy and singing.
The glory of Lebanon shall be given to it,
the majesty of Carmel and Sharon.
They shall see the glory of the Lord,
the majesty of our God...
For waters shall break forth in the wilderness,
and streams in the desert;
the burning sand shall become a pool,
and the thirsty ground springs of water;
the haunt of jackals shall become a swamp,
the grass shall become reeds and rushes.
A highway shall be there,
and it shall be called the Holy Way;
the unclean shall not travel on it,
but it shall be for God's people;
no traveller, not even fools, shall go astray.
No lion shall be there,
nor shall any ravenous beast come up on it;
they shall not be found there,
but the redeemed shall walk there.
And the ransomed of the Lord shall return,
and come to Zion with singing;
everlasting joy shall be upon their heads;
they shall obtain joy and gladness,
and sorrow and sighing shall flee away.

ISAIAH 35:1–2, 6b–10

The 'wilderness' features prominently in the Bible. Anyone who has visited Israel and the West Bank will have seen the Judean wilderness, an area of stone-strewn scrubland, hilly, hot and in-hospitable, stretching eastwards from the outskirts of modern Jerusalem down to the Jordan valley and southwards to the Dead Sea. It is not, by the standards of world geography, a very large wilderness or desert—not even as large by a long way as the desert wilderness through which the Israelites picked their slow way from Egypt to Canaan. But this particular wilderness has as much mytho-logical significance in the Bible as geographical. It's not the size of this or any other wilderness that matters, but its symbolic role, representing the place of solitude, of challenge, of divine revelation, of the ultimate human test.

After all, the history of Israel was forged in the heat of the desert—not this one, but the wilderness of Sinai. Here, Moses stood at the burning bush and heard the call to go and lead the Hebrew people out of Egypt across its burning wastes. Here, the people thirsted, and were given fresh water. Here, they were hungry, and were fed with manna from heaven. Here, they were given the law, carved in stone from the barren hills. Here, they rebelled, and were punished for their rebellion. Out of the wilderness they eventually emerged to take possession of their own Promised Land, flowing with milk and honey, true, but also within its borders encompassing its own wilderness, to serve as a perpetual reminder of the place where their nationhood was born.

So the wilderness took its place in the story of Israel, always as the place of encounter with God, a place where a person could be tested and tried—and then perhaps called to God's service, or called back to it, like Elijah (1 Kings 19:4). Significantly, it was a voice in the wilderness that would herald the coming of the Messiah (Isaiah 40:3). When Jesus was to come, it was in this same wilderness that John the Baptist preached his message of preparation by repentance. It was here that Jesus was 'tested' by Satan and in which later, like a latter-day Moses, he fed the people with loaves and fish—though whether the feeding of the five thousand really took place in the desert, as the Gospel writers assert (Luke 9:12–17), or whether it was simply a lonely place which spoke to them of the wilderness in which God's people were miraculously fed long ago (Exodus 16), may be a matter of conjecture. Later, the apostle Paul tested his call by spending three years in the wilderness (Galatians 1:17–18).

In the passage from Isaiah 35, we see the wilderness transformed. This was the ultimate expression of hope—that God himself would take what was dead and barren and breathe new life into it. Here would take place the coming of the golden age: the dry lands would produce crops; the God of judgment would become a God of blessing; water would break out in the desert, and reeds and rushes would grow there. Not only would the land be healed, but the people, too: the blind would see, the deaf hear, the lame walk and the dumb sing for joy. This is a vision of salvation—the complete healing of the natural order, humans, animals, plants and nature itself restored to its full and original glory. And only God could do it; only the creator could re-create.

The spiritual lesson of the wilderness is one that the Hebrew Bible often emphasizes. 'Remember the long way that the Lord your God has led you these forty years in the wilderness, in order to humble you, testing you to know what was in your heart, whether or not you would keep his commandments. He humbled you by letting you hunger, then by feeding you with manna, with which neither you nor your ancestors were acquainted, in order to make you understand that one does not live by bread alone, but by every word that comes from the mouth of the Lord.' (Deuteronomy 8:2–3). The wilderness experience, in other words, is essentially a positive one. By removing all the normal human props, it brings us face to face with God, and in that encounter we learn in a more profound way to trust him and obey what he says. Indeed, we learn the deepest lesson of all, that 'things' are not what makes life good, but knowing the will of God and doing it—living 'by every word that comes from the mouth of the Lord'.

A reflection

In the wilderness, we can learn lessons that it is simply impossible to learn anywhere else.

38

WISDOM

'Where then does wisdom come from?
And where is the place of understanding?
It is hidden from the eyes of all living,
and concealed from the birds of the air.
Abaddon and Death say,
"We have heard a rumour of it
with our ears."
God understands the way to it,
and he knows its place.
For he looks to the ends of the earth,
and sees everything under the heavens...
And he said to humankind,
"Truly, the fear of the Lord, that is wisdom;
and to depart from evil is understanding."'

JOB 28:20–24, 28

Three books in the Hebrew scriptures are usually designated 'wisdom literature'. They are Job, Proverbs and Ecclesiastes. But the notion of 'wisdom' as both a gift of God and a means to live well runs through very much of the Bible. There is a strong wisdom element in the Psalms, for instance (see Psalms 1, 19, 49, 73, 111 and 112, among others) and in many of the biblical narratives, such as the one relating how Solomon received the gift of wisdom in answer to prayer (1 Kings 3:11–14). Indeed, wisdom was a revered concept in many of the cultures of the ancient world, and Egypt and Mesopotamia had writings very similar in style to the wisdom books of the Old Testament.

'Wisdom', in this sense, is judgment, knowledge and under-

134

standing, especially of the ways in which the divine will interacts with the human one. These writings raise some of the most profound philosophical questions about such matters as the origin of evil, the meaning of suffering, the mystery of death, the inequality of fate and destiny in people's lives, and the cultivation of a life of virtue. Some do this in dialogue form (like Job), some in the form of proverbs and wise sayings (Proverbs), some in lessons or sermons (Ecclesiastes), and some by means of stories, metaphor and allegories, sometimes written as hymns or poems (see, for instance, Ezekiel 28 or Proverbs 8 and 9). Some would see similar elements in such narratives as the story of the temptation and fall (Genesis 2 and 3) or the exemplary tale of Joseph and his brothers (Genesis 37—50).

What all of these writings have in common is an exploration of the great themes of wisdom: cause and effect (especially in human behaviour and God's response to it), the order of the universe and the nature of time as elements of God's creation and the limits to human power and authority. The refrain runs constantly through wisdom literature: 'the fear of the Lord is the beginning of wisdom' (see, for instance, Job 28:28; Proverbs 1:7, 29; 9:10; 14:27; 15:16; 19:23; Ecclesiastes 12:13). True wisdom (understanding), in other words, has its origins in a reverent acceptance of God's will and purposes. We can seek to understand, but we can never be part of the divine knowledge which shapes the whole of creation and everything that happens in it. Why do suffering and death not respect virtue and piety? How does the mind of God reveal itself in human affairs and in the material world? At the end of the book of Job, after all the arguments and counter-arguments, Job can rejoice that God can be seen and his wisdom recognized even though it is literally and always beyond human understanding (42:2–6). That is, in essence, the wisdom that comes from 'fearing' God—standing in awe of him, we might say. The wise person does not judge God, but allows God's wisdom to judge him or her.

If the theme of wisdom as springing from reverence for God is one great refrain of the wisdom writings, the other is surely the notion of the 'two ways', the two paths human beings can choose.

One is the way of evil and the other is the way of goodness. This theme is set out right at the beginning of the Psalter: 'Happy are those who do not follow the advice of the wicked, or take the path that sinners tread, or sit in the seat of scoffers... for the Lord watches over the way of the righteous, but the way of the wicked will perish' (Psalm 1:1, 6). This fundamental choice, which brings as a consequence blessing or disaster, runs right through Proverbs and is central to the Jewish understanding of virtue. The good person chooses the good; the evil person chooses the evil. It is interesting to find it expounded vividly in the teaching of Jesus (Matthew 7:13, 14). In this understanding, human choice and divine will are either on a collision or a collusion course, and from Eden onwards the message is spelt out in stark terms. To seek God's will and do it is true wisdom, and also the path to the good life.

All of this is based on a profound theological truth. Because God guides and orders the whole created universe—and everything that happens is part of his purpose, even if not directly caused by him—discovering and obeying God's will is crucial to human well-being. It is, in fact, true wisdom.

A reflection

For Paul, the 'world did not know God through wisdom', but Christ crucified has revealed 'the power of God and the wisdom of God' (1 Corinthians 1:21, 24). How could this be? Why, because 'God's foolishness is wiser than human wisdom' (v. 25)— the suffering and death of Jesus were a revelation of the will and purpose of the creator, no less.

39

WORSHIP

When Solomon had ended his prayer, fire came down from heaven and consumed the burnt-offering and the sacrifices; and the glory of the Lord filled the temple. The priests could not enter the house of the Lord, because the glory of the Lord filled the Lord's house. When all the people of Israel saw the fire come down and the glory of the Lord on the temple, they bowed down on the pavement with their faces to the ground, and worshipped and gave thanks to the Lord, saying, 'For he is good, for his steadfast love endures for ever.'

2 CHRONICLES 7:1–3

We have already considered worship in the context of joyful praise (under 'Praise'). Now we are to reflect on the role that worship played in the life of the Old Testament—worship, that is, as a formal and organized activity centred on the temple. Worship itself, as we have seen, seems to be a fundamental characteristic of human nature. Indeed, if we have no god to worship we invent one, whether it be a football team, a car, or a particular place. For the Israelites, formed into a people by the experience of the Exodus, worship was a corporate (we might even say 'tribal') activity, which served to define them as God's people, bound to him in covenant love and commitment, and offering him true worship. In a formal sense, that worship was forged in the heat of the wilderness as they gathered day by day in the tent of meeting, later to become the tabernacle and later still the temple.

It would be wrong, however, to think of worship as something the people offered to God, without recognizing that true worship is also a movement of God towards his people. In the passage above, for instance—the vivid account of the consecration of Solomon's temple—the whole act of worship is triggered by two actions of the Lord. He sent fire from heaven to consume the burnt-offering on the altar, and then 'the glory of the Lord filled the temple'. It is hard to imagine what this phenomenon would have involved, but obviously it was visible to human eyes, because it prevented the priests from entering the 'house of the Lord'. It may have been a spectacular blaze of light from the sun which blinded their eyes, or a fiery consequence of the conflagration on the altar. What is clear is that this was taken by the king, the priests and the people as a sign calling them to bow down, with their faces to the ground, and worship. In fact, the most usual word in Hebrew for worship literally means 'to bow in reverence'.

The worship of Israel, in this formal sense, was thereafter more or less confined to the temple precincts until the time of the exile. Taken far away from the appointed centre of divine worship, the Jewish people began to meet in 'prayer centres', which became known as 'synagogues' (the word simply means 'meeting-place' or 'assembly'). After the destruction of the temple in AD70, the Jews of the Dispersion have gathered in synagogues, mainly for the teaching of the law and for prayers. Without a temple, there could be no legitimate centre for the offering of sacrifices, which were central to the whole idea of worship and thanksgiving until that point.

The outstanding note of temple worship, as we can see from this passage, was awe. There can be little doubt that anyone entering the courts of Solomon's temple, or the later temple built by Herod, would have been overwhelmed with a sense of majesty, splendour and reverence. The praises of Israel, as we have seen, were often explosive and noisy, joyful and exuberant. The worship of Israel, on the other hand, was characterized by an awestruck silence. The great pillars and arches, the vestments of the priests, the carvings and ornaments, the curtains and fittings, all were calculated to bring the worshippers to their knees; to 'worship the Lord in holy splendour' (Psalm 96:9).

This experience is captured in several psalms. 'Awesome is God in his sanctuary, the God of Israel; he gives power and strength to his people' (Psalm 68:35). Perhaps more tellingly, in Psalm 63 the writer cries out to God in a time of great spiritual need and distress: 'O God, you are my God, I seek you, my soul thirsts for you; my flesh faints for you, as in a dry and weary land where there is no water' (v. 1). He finds the answer when he enters the temple: 'So I have looked upon you in the sanctuary, beholding your power and glory. Because your steadfast love is better than life, my lips will praise you. So I will bless you as long as I live; I will lift up my hands and call on your name' (vv. 2–4).

In some way, God's 'power and glory', revealed in the setting of the place of worship, spoke to the psalmist of his 'loving-kindness', his covenant love. In response to that revelation, he determines to bless the Lord as long as he lives, to lift up his hands (in adoration and worship) and to call on God's name in prayer.

A very good way to sample the true flavour of the worship of Israel is to read the beautiful 'songs of ascents'—Psalms 120 to 134. These were probably sung by pilgrims as they made their way up the long temple slope towards the great gates and, as well as being wonderful poetry, even in translation, capture both the joy and the solemnity of worship. Some sing from hearts heavy with need and anxiety: 'Out of the depths I cry to you, O Lord'—the famous De profundis (130:1). Some speak of God's presence and protection: 'I lift up my eyes to the hills—from where will my help come? My help comes from the Lord' (121:1–2). Some speak of the glad expectation of blessing: 'I was glad when they said to me, "Let us go to the house of the Lord"' (122:1). Others are songs of trust: 'As the mountains surround Jerusalem, so the Lord surrounds his people, from this time on and for evermore' (125:2), or of quiet hope: 'I have calmed and quieted my soul, like a weaned child with its mother' (131:2). There is something wonderful about the way that particular image can cross the centuries of human experience.

All of this helps to underline the profound truth that there is no impervious barrier between reverence and intimacy. The same people who sang their way to the gates of the temple may well have fallen into awestruck silence by what they saw and felt as they entered the sanctuary of God. The God who speaks by fire, in other words, also speaks by a 'still, small voice'.

A reflection

Is it possible that modern Christians sometimes devalue the whole idea of 'worship' by attaching the word to all manner of activities that may fall short of awe and wonder? There may be a kind of dumbing-down involved, if that which we call 'worship' does not include this element which lay at the heart of Israel's devotion: a deep and reverent awe at the greatness and holiness of the One into whose presence we come.

40

YAHWEH

But Moses said to God, 'If I come to the Israelites and say to them,
"The God of your ancestors has sent me to you," and they ask me,
"What is his name?" what shall I say to them?' God said to Moses,
'I am who I am.' He said further, 'Thus you shall say to the
Israelites, "I am has sent me to you."' God also said to Moses,
'Thus you shall say to the Israelites, "The Lord, the God of your
ancestors, the God of Abraham, the God of Isaac, and the God of
Jacob, has sent me to you": This is my name for ever, and this my
title for all generations.'

EXODUS 3:13–15

For this last chapter, we consider the most common proper noun
in the Old Testament, though you won't find it in most English
translations (the exception is the Jerusalem Bible). 'Yahweh' occurs
almost six thousand times, generally translated in English as 'the
LORD', the capital letters in most English translations distinguishing
it from other titles of the deity. Christians are probably most familiar
with it in its abbreviated form '*ya*', as in 'hallelujah' ('praise Yahweh').
It is safe to say that the name is the clue to the whole of the Hebrew
scriptures, yet there almost seems to be a conspiracy to hide it
from us!

If we assume that there were at least two strands of composition
or editing in the creation of these scriptures as we now have them
(and many people identify four), it is possible to find evidence for it
in the use of the divine name. Scholars have identified an editor or
team of editors whom they label 'J'—the German initial of Yahweh.
They also identify at least one other such team, whom they label 'P',
for 'priestly'—the scriptures which are most concerned with the

temple and its sacrifices and rituals. The 'J' editor uses the name Yahweh before the Flood. Indeed, during the lifetime of Adam and Eve 'people began to invoke the name of the LORD [Yahweh]' (Genesis 4:26b). The 'P' editor dates its first use to the confrontation between Moses and Pharaoh: 'God also spoke to Moses and said to him: "I am the LORD. I appeared to Abraham, Isaac, and Jacob as God Almighty, but by my name 'The LORD' I did not make myself known to them"' (Exodus 6:2–3).

Such details need not bother the general reader of the Old Testament. By whatever means, the people of Israel learnt that their God was not simply a tribal deity. He is the source and creator of all that exists, and he himself is eternal. As the passage at the head of this chapter makes clear, the God of Abraham, Isaac and Jacob is not to be confined to a period of history. He has no beginning and no ending, but simply is: 'I am'. All of his creatures have a past and a present, but God is simply always present tense.

The name Yahweh, though almost as mysterious in meaning as the origins of the title, is probably connected with the Hebrew verb 'to be' (hwh). God simply exists and is the source of everything else that exists. Thus, it is the perfect title for the eternal creator.

As time passed, increasing reverence and also fear of blasphemy, especially on the part of Israel's enemies, meant that the name was never spoken aloud. It was usually replaced in public by 'Adonai', 'my Lord'. When, in the course of time, vowels were added to the consonants which had previously been the form of Hebrew writing, the vowels of that word were added to the consonants of the divinely revealed name, YHWH, as a kind of warning to those reading aloud to say 'Adonai' rather than 'Yahweh'. From this, Christian translators wrongly created a hybrid word 'Jehovah'.

If we leave the etymology and turn to the theology, we shall begin to touch on the true heart of Israelite religion. Because Yahweh was not a tribal god, but the eternal creator, he was intrinsically different (they would have said 'superior to') the gods of the other nations. He was to be worshipped not because he could do things for them, though he could, but because of who he is. The name which was revealed to Moses at the burning bush may be enigmatic, but it certainly speaks of an infinite personhood. 'I am who I am' could be translated 'I am what I am' or even 'I will be what I will be'—here is a God who is personal and infinite, who could speak to his people, and on whom they could rely not just for the present but for the future, stretching into infinity. As we have seen, the divine title embraces this concept of pure being: God *is*.

This incident at the burning bush also revealed that the infinite, personal God is one who cares, who can feel pain, sorrow, indignation, sympathy. 'Then the Lord said, "I have observed the misery of my people who are in Egypt; I have heard their cry on account of their taskmasters. Indeed, I know their sufferings, and I have come down to deliver them from the Egyptians, and to bring them up out of that land to a good and broad land, a land flowing with milk and honey… The cry of the Israelites has now come to me; I have also seen how the Egyptians oppress them".' (Exodus 3:7–9).

If we put those elements together, we have a wonderful picture of the God of the Bible. He is infinite, without beginning or ending, the source of light, life and love. He is personal—which does not mean that he is human, but that the highest human attribute, which is personhood, comes from him: we are 'made in his image' (Genesis 1:27). And he is good, a God who not only is to be loved, but who loves and, like a shepherd, cares for and protects his people. This is the God of Abraham, Isaac and Jacob, but he is also the God and Father of the Lord Jesus Christ—and there is nothing inconsistent in that.

A reflection

Some people read the Old Testament and see only mayhem, violence, cruelty and bloodshed. Some look more deeply, and see behind its stories, its poetry and its human misunderstandings of God's purposes the portrait of a wise and gracious God who embraces within his nature such diverse concepts as holiness, mercy, power, justice and love.

Above all, he is faithful, the 'rock', the 'tower of defence', the one who does not lose his grip on history and is not subject to change and chance. The people of Israel were called to serve such a God, a God of faithfulness and justice, of infinite mercy and love. Nothing has really changed. So are we.